THE DISINTEGRATION OF FORM

IN THE ARTS

Also by Erich Kahler

MAN THE MEASURE

THE TOWER AND THE ABYSS

THE MEANING OF HISTORY

OUT OF THE LABYRINTH

The Disintegration of Form

in the Arts

BY

ERICH KAHLER

GEORGE BRAZILLER · NEW YORK

THE DISINTEGRATION OF FORM
IN THE ARTS

THREE LECTURES DELIVERED AT
PRINCETON UNIVERSITY
APRIL-MAY, 1967
AND AT
THE STATE UNIVERSITY OF NEW YORK AT STONY BROOK
DECEMBER, 1967

For information address the publisher:
George Braziller, Inc.
One Park Avenue
New York, New York 10016

Library of Congress Catalog Card Number: 68–12888
Designed by Jennie R. Bush
Printed in the United States of America

Contents

List of Illustrations
vii

I
THE FORMS OF FORM
1

II
THE PRELIMINARY STAGES
OF DISINTEGRATION
25

III
THE TRIUMPH OF INCOHERENCE
71

References
127

Index
131

LIST OF ILLUSTRATIONS

page

Pablo Picasso, "Abstractions of a Bull" (Six
    Lithographs)   52–53
Jackson Pollock, "Number 8" (1950)   54
Mark Rothko, "Number 19" (1958)   55
Barnett Newman, "Abraham" (1949)   56
Ad Reinhardt, "Abstract Painting" (1960–61)   57
Georges Braque, "The Program" (1913)   58
Kurt Schwitters, "Cherry Picture" (1921)   59
Joan Miró, "Poetic Object" (1936)   60
Louise Nevelson, "Royal Tide I" (1960)   61
Alberto Burri, "Composition 8" (1953)   62
Jasper Johns, "Flashlight" (1960)   63
Armand Arman, "Glug-Glug" (1961)   64
Yayoi Kusama, "Air Mail Stickers" (1962)   65
Nobuaki Kojima, figure (untitled, 1964)   66
George Segal, "Couple on a Bed" (1965)   67
Tadasky, "A-101" (1964)   68
Benjamin Cunningham, "Equivocation" (1964)   69
Franz Mon, "Schreibmaschinentextbild"   113

[vii]

Franz Mon, "Abstraktion"   *114*

Bradley Tomlin, "Number 9: In Praise of Gertrude
    Stein" (1950)   *115*

Ben Shahn, "Who Is God?"   *116*

Ben Shahn, untitled composition   *117*

Mark Tobey, "Sumi Still Life" (1957)   *118*

Paul Klee, "Pinselzeichnung"   *119*

Guillaume Apollinaire, "Paysage"   *120*

Guillaume Apollinaire, "Il Pleut"   *121*

Klaus Peter Dienst, "Kalligramm"   *122*

John Cage, "Notations for Chance Composition"   *123*

Carlfriedrich Claus, "6 Phasen von 52"   *124–125*

Diter Rot, untitled calligram   *126*

THE DISINTEGRATION OF FORM

IN THE ARTS

I

The Forms of Form

$\mathcal{W}$HAT I want to discuss in these lectures does not concern art alone, or art per se. To be sure, I will try to determine what basically is going on in the arts of our day, and to look for a common tendency in the anarchically multifold artistic endeavors we are witnessing. My principal purpose, however, is to put these movements in a broader perspective, to show them, *first,* as results of general social and civilizational developments, *second,* as symptoms of our present human condition, and *third,* as agents prominently contributing to what I consider an extremely dangerous trend of events. Art is a mode of human expression, or, to avoid the term "expression" which, as you will see, has assumed a problematic character for some avant-garde movements, let us take it simply as a peculiar manifestation of human existence. As such, art, just as life itself, is not compartmentalized, and what happens to artistic form seriously affects the human form, the form of man.

[3]

I speak of artistic form and of human form. This calls for an initial clarification of what precisely is to be understood by "form," a term that is often used very loosely and vaguely. Commonly, form is identified with *shape*. In this broadest, most palpable sense, anything bounded would have some form, and "form" would be equivalent to discernible bounds. But this appears to me a very superficial, purely external conception of form. Shape may be the outer aspect of form, but seen in itself, it is not form. Only inasmuch as shape constitutes the outer appearance of a *structure,* which means, of an inner organization, an inner organizational coherence of a bounded entity, does it belong to form. Form, accordingly, can be defined roughly as *structure manifesting itself in shape.*

A lake, for instance, has shape, but it has no structure, and it seems to me therefore not quite correct to speak of the form of a lake. But any organic body, any living creature has form, indeed *is* form. And the human being, which extends far beyond physical existence into realms of psychic, intellectual and spiritual reflection, and thus, through memory and awareness of identity, also into the dimension of time, that is, into history—the human being is up to this point the most highly structured being, the most advanced natural form of all. In this sense of a being, coherent beyond physical perceptibility, coherent through a reflective awareness encompassing his psychic, cultural, and temporal existence, we can speak of *human form.* And,

[4]

let me add, this applies not only to the human individual, whose shape is physically perceptible; it applies as well to the *genus humanum* as a whole, as a specific organic form which, if we believe our most recent findings, made its appearance about two and a half million years ago. Since its development has come to transcend its physical and physically perceptible bounds, its structure and shape can be grasped only by intellectual means.

I am fully aware that with such a view I am in striking conflict with that scientistic reliance on sensory validation and verifiability of facts which is overwhelmingly predominant today. It is noteworthy, however, that even in the basic sciences sensory verification has to be achieved today in a more and more indirect, indeed instrumentally abstract way, and at certain points, it has arrived at apparently impenetrable limits.

Now in these lectures we have to deal primarily with *artistic form* and its implications for the human form. Artistic form is structure and shape created by a human act. This may indeed be accepted as a preliminary distinction of art: *art is form created by a human, intellectual act.*

But if we want to explore the meaning of the present trends in the arts and to establish the criteria indispensable for such a task, we have to delve a little deeper into the nature of form. And in attempting to do this, it seems to me, we cannot find a better point of departure than the first, classical standard of form as put down by Aristotle in his *Poetics*. In doing so, we may disregard, as irrelevant for our purpose, Aristotle's thesis that the motive and function of art consists in imitation, however his concept of *mimesis* may be interpreted. Nor does it seem to me required any longer that we dispose of the old aesthetic dichotomy of form and content. It may be taken for granted by now, I hope, that "content" and "form" are but two aspects of one and the same thing—the *what* determines the *how*, and, conversely, the *how* does not exist without the *what* which it is meant to convey. This is by no means invalidated by the observation that more recently the problem of how to render the bewildering complexity of our reality has become the very subject matter of certain works of art. Such apparent "formalization" actually does not mean a prevalence of "form" over "content"; it means the presentation in a work of art of the artist's struggle with his task—a kind of artistic epistemology. Besides, it will be seen that this ultimately leads to the dissolution not only of what has been considered as "content," but of artistic form altogether. "Form" breaks down with its substratum, for it is inseparably one with its substratum.

In the passage of the *Poetics* which concerns us here, Aristotle speaks of beauty, but for it we may, I think, legitimately, substitute perfection of form. "Beauty," he says, "depends on these qualities: size and order. Hence an extremely minute creature cannot be beautiful to us, for our view (of the whole) is confounded when it is formed in an almost infinitesimal moment of time. Nor could a creature of too vast dimensions be beautiful to us . . . for in that case our view could not take all of the object in at once and we do not see the unity of the whole. In the same way, then, as an inanimate object . . . or a living creature must be easily taken in by the eye (*eusynopton*, easily synoptic), just so must the plot of a tragedy have a proper length, so that the whole may be easily embraced by the memory. . . ." And now comes what establishes his standard of artistic form: "As in the other arts, so in poetry the object is a unit; therefore, in a tragedy, the plot, representing an organically united action, must be an identical whole, the structural order of the incidents being such that transposing or removing any one of them will dislocate and disorganize the whole; for a thing whose presence or absence makes no perceptible difference is not an organic part of the whole."[1]

For Aristotle, then, a work of art is a closely coherent and consistent whole; it is, or rather should be, what Socrates in Plato's *Phaedrus* correspondingly demands of discourse: a unit "like a living creature." It is, we may conclude, *a living thing, created by a human, intellectual act.*

This classical standard of artistic form has retained its validity throughout the ages; it has been followed by Vergil,* by Dante, by the French classicists and symbolists,

* George E. Duckworth, *Structural Patterns and Proportions in Vergil's Aeneis* (Michigan University Press, 1962).

by Goethe, and Heinrich von Kleist. It has been, with increasing flexibility and complexity, the aim of conscious
artistry in the last century. It is the pursuit of this form
which made "the joy and the agony" of Flaubert; it is what
Henry James called "the sublime economy of art." It is
what Flaubert meant when he said, "*les chef-d'oeuvres sont
bêtes*," "masterpieces are dumb," that is to say, they are so
self-centered, so at rest in themselves, so rounded and
closed, that nothing can enter and affect them from without. It is what Yeats must have had in mind when he said:
"Our words must seem inevitable." It is what dominates
the work of Cézanne, of Matisse: "In a picture," Matisse
said,[2] "every part will play the role conferred upon it, be it
principal or secondary. All that is not useful in the picture
is detrimental," and again "[every drawing] will have a
necessary relation to its format" and "when I have found
the relationship of all the tones, the result must be a
living harmony of tones, a harmony not unlike that of a
musical composition." Cézanne's recommendation to "treat
nature by the cylinder, the sphere, the cone, everything in
proper perspective so that each side of an object, or a plane,
is directed towards a central point" corresponds exactly to
Tolstoi's demand that every work of art "should have a
kind of focus." And this focus must not be completely
explainable in words: "the content [of a true work of art]
can in its entirety be expressed only by itself." Chekhov's
stories, Ibsen's plays, little as they may outwardly show it,

reveal themselves upon a closer look as prodigies of meticulous construction. Chekhov once said: "If in the first act of a play a rifle is seen hanging on the wall, it has to shoot in the last act." Finally, pioneering novels of our century, Joyce's *Ulysses,* Gide's *Faux Monnayeurs,* Thomas Mann's *Doctor Faustus,* Hermann Broch's *Tod des Vergil,* Elisabeth Langgässer's *Das unauslöschliche Siegel,* among others —most of them the result of years of intent labor, of weighing and balancing every move and word—such works have reached an extreme of organic construction: they are, in point of fact, vastly expanded and amplified paradigms of the Aristotelian concept of artistic form. There are among such works some whose strict organization has more musical character, others whose order is rather of a pictorial kind; some, unfolding their organic sequences and correspondences within the stretch of absolute time, that is, within one, homogeneous time, others in which time itself has become an element of artistic interplay, in which different, relative modes of time mingle and intertwine so as to convey a sense of transcending simultaneity, of a supratemporal space. Virginia Woolf's *Orlando,* Thomas Mann's *Magic Mountain* and *Doctor Faustus,* Butor's *Emploi du temps,* Styron's *Lie Down in Darkness,* Uwe Johnson's *Mutmassungen über Jakob* are examples of the second kind.

In music, accomplished form becomes evident in the manifold, more and more complex, dialectically dynamic, and yet supratemporal coherence of compositions. Another requisite of artistic economy, *conciseness,* has been stressed by Anton von Webern. "By art," he writes, "I understand the capacity to put an idea into the clearest, simplest, and that is, most graspable (*fasslichste*) form. . . . [Thus] Beethoven drafted the main theme of the first movement of his *Eroica* so many times as to get it finally to a degree of simplicity comparable to a sentence of the Lord's Prayer."

There are two kinds of simplicity: a naïve, pre-conscious simplicity, untouched by the experience of the immense complexity of the phenomena of life, and a post-conscious simplicity which is the result of an extreme artistic effort to master this complexity, and in whose accomplishment we still sense the vibration of this experience and this laboring. It is in this awareness, and this struggle to cope with it, rudimentary as it may be, that true artistic endeavor begins.

There are, however, and there always have been, works which are recognized and admired as works of art although they do not seem to fit into this classical concept; whose creators, either by disregard or by intent, have transgressed the basic standards of rounded form. Think of the modern novel in its beginnings, the boundless novels of the Baroque, *Don Quixote, Gargantua, Simplizissimus;* of the great English novels of the eighteenth century, and later, the profuse narratives of Balzac, of Dickens, of Proust. Think of the paintings of mannerism, or of Bosch and

Breughel. And how about some of the greatest, yet some-
how loose, lopsided plays of Shakespeare? Or romantic,
expressionist, surrealist poetry? Are we to consider all such
works just faulty, unfinished, fragmentary attempts which
failed to attain to true form? In most of them we do not
even discover a conscious intention to achieve a closed form.
Their creators simply let go, or deliberately go beyond any
restrictive bounds. And yet, we feel compelled to regard
these creations as great works of art. Now what is it, we
must ask, that compels us to do so?

To satisfy, or rather to evade, this query, the term "open
form" has been invented—as far as I can see, by the Swiss
art historian, Heinrich Wölfflin. In his book, *Kunst-
geschichtliche Grundbegriffe* (Basic Concepts of Art History), 1915, he contrasted "open form" with "closed
form." The concept of "open form," however, vague as
it is, raises more basic problems. "Closed form" has only
one distinct meaning, so precise, in fact, that it seems a
redundancy. Being closed within itself like an organic
being implies the perfection of form; and, as applied to
artistic work, it indicates an effort that is by definition
artistic. But a work composed in "open form" is not necessarily a truly artistic one; all sorts of extraneous aims may
prevail in it, emotions, purposes, conventions, rhetorics of
persuasion, or simply an uncontrolled enjoyment of depic-
tion and narration. So a work constituting an open form
requires an additional specification as to whether and how

far it may be considered artistic, and what it is that makes it artistic. When we look carefully we shall find that even in works with "open form" it is some at least half-conscious effort toward perfection of form, which means closed form, that makes them artistic.

Any work of art has more than one dimension. Its artistic quality makes itself felt in the dimensions of breadth, length, and depth, and indeed even in the dimension of time.

The structure, the inner coherence of a work of art extends, with its ramifications and correspondences of motifs, first of all, on its more manifest level, in the dimensions of breadth and length. The dimension of depth takes it to other levels, and that implies additional fields of correlation and what may be singled out as another, no less essential attribute of a work of art: its *symbolic quality,* its moving simultaneously on different levels.

It is this quality which Thomas Hardy seems to have had in mind when he said: "The whole secret of fiction and the drama—in the constructional part—lies in the adjustment of things unusual to things eternal and universal. The writer who knows exactly how exceptional and how non-exceptional his events should be made, possesses the key to the art."[3]

What Hardy indicates, quite rightly, I think, is that the essence of literary art consists in a *relationship between two levels of existence.* But I would argue that it is neither the relationship of "exceptional" to "non-exceptional," nor the "adjustment" of the "unusual" to the "universal" that makes the difference; it is rather the *relationship* of the *specific,* be it exceptional or non-exceptional, to the *universal;* and not an "adjustment," but an *accomplished identity* of the particular with the general. No single event has artistic value unless it has generally human relevance. The true artist reaches beyond the phenomenal level, the surface level, on which both, the usual and the unusual, the exceptional and the non-exceptional take place; he drives an occurrence or a situation into a depth of intensity where it is every human being's concern and potentiality. (The commonly "usual," "non-exceptional" is by no means coincident with the humanly universal; it is more often its very opposite, a specific peripheral conventionality, like a ritual, a national custom, a class standard, a fashion.)

Both the commonly usual and the quite unusual may, in the grasp of an artist, assume a general import. The classical example of the first case is Flaubert's *Un coeur simple,* a story in which something quite ordinary becomes the ordinary par excellence. A most trivial course of events, a most inconspicuous character and destiny are raised to a paradigm of the sublimity of the humble, more Christian than anything explicitly so. This is achieved by symbolic concentration, and, accordingly, this story is, like all other works of Flaubert, a model of "closed form"; it is so closely knit, it is done with such perfect accuracy and interaction

[13]

of parts that not the minutest detail is superfluous or out of place. Here it is the concentration of closed form itself that constitutes the symbolic quality, the identity of two levels of existence.

Just the opposite in every respect are the stories of Balzac, which depict exceptional, indeed eccentric happenings, characters, careers, in a loose and prodigal manner. They are, on the surface level, striking examples of "open form." But by their emotional intensity and by their very affluence, even prolixity, of description, they achieve what masters of the closed form achieve through the perfection of artistic economy: symbolic depth, and that means, broadly human relevance. They show how within open form, one could even say *by means* of open form, a symbolic conformity between two levels of existence can be attained that equals the artistic effect of a completely rounded form.

The contrast between closed form and such open form as achieves an interlevel, symbolic conformity is exemplified in poetry by the conciseness of the verse of Baudelaire, Mallarmé, Hopkins, Valéry as against the impetuous flow of Walt Whitman's or Dylan Thomas' free rhapsodies.

This interlevel, symbolic conformity is *one* mode of artistic form that occurs within an open form. There are others. Let us take an extreme case of open form, Henry Miller's *Tropic of Cancer*. As a whole, it is certainly a chaotic book, exceptional in this respect even among the generally ebullient and unorganized narratives of this great author. What makes it artistic, what raises it beyond its entirely private records and sheer obscenities is the rendering of a scene, a scenery, an atmosphere, with a passionate, sweeping vigor of truth, it is its showing in every instance and instant the *multiformity of life* with its harsh contrasts, the funny with the wretched, the blooming in the decay, the spark of love and charm in the whore. There are, within the wild flux of effusion, islands of wholeness, such as this:

> Wandering along the Seine at night, wandering and wandering, and going mad with the beauty of it, the trees leaning to, the broken images in the water, the rush of the current under the bloody lights of the bridges, the women sleeping in doorways, sleeping on newspapers, sleeping in the rain; everywhere the musty porches of the cathedrals and beggars and lice and old hags full of St. Vitus' dance; pushcarts stacked up like wine barrels in the side streets, the smell of berries in the market-place and the old church surrounded with vegetables and blue arc-lights, the gutters slippery with garbage and women in satin pumps staggering through the filth and vermin at the end of an all-night souse. . . .[4]

Such impression and expression of the many-sided *totality of existence,* such delight in its newly-felt sub- and suprarational coherence is an achievement of the rarified sensibility of our age. Wherever it appears, even in the midst of entirely uncontrolled narrative, there is artistic form of a closed and rounded nature.

[15]

This may lead to the paradox of *accomplished form made up of the very amorphous,* of the debris of our fragmented life, as it appears in some recent collages and assemblages or in lyrics like those of the exquisite, most form-conscious German poet, Gottfried Benn. His poetry conveys, is intended to convey, a feeling of the disruption of organic being, of the shambles of our individual existence—and to convey it in an impeccable form. A particular strictness of stanza, meter, and rhyme serves here to accentuate the harsh disruptions they tell. Benn's whole work, a despairing attempt at integration of unresolved discord, may be seen implied in his poem *Schutt,* "Rubble," of which I quote two stanzas:

> Schutt, alle Trümmer
> liegen morgens so bloss
> wahr ist immer nur eines:
> du und das Grenzenlos—
> trinke und alle Schatten
> hängen die Lippe ins Glas
> fütterst du dein Ermatten—
> lass—!
>
> Komm, und drängt sich mit Brüsten
> Eutern zu Tête à tête
> letztes Lebensgelüsten,
> lass, es ist zu spät.
> Komm, alle Skalen tosen
> Spuk, Entformungsgefühl—
> komm, es fallen wie Rosen
> Götter und Götterspiel.

Wreckage—all the rubble
lies at morning so bare
true is only and always:
you and the boundless are there—
drink, and all the shadows
hang a lip in your glass
will you feed your weakening—
leave it and pass—!

Come, if last life's hankerings
press into tête-à-tête
with chest's and breasts' nipples,
leave it, it is too late.
Come, all the scales rumble
ghosts, sense of decay—
come, like roses tumble
gods, and the gods' play.

Generally, in recent poetry and in certain novelistic
works of the twentieth century, form, expressing the
totality of existence, reaches the fastest, transrational concentration: all elaborative, explanatory bridges are broken.
"Sometimes," T. S. Eliot remarks in his preface to Djuna
Barnes' *Nightwood*, "in a phrase the characters spring to
life so suddenly that one is taken aback, as if one had
touched a wax-work figure and discovered that it was a live
policeman." The flash-like abruptness of metaphorical connections opens a depth and subtlety of precision such as has
never been attained before. Here are, from *Nightwood*, a
few examples of characterization of a woman:

Her movements were slightly headlong and sideways:
slow, clumsy and yet graceful, the ample gait of the night-
watch. . . . She was gracious and yet fading, like an old
statue in a garden, that symbolizes the weather through
which it has endured, and is not so much the work of man
as the work of wind and rain and the herd of the seasons,
and, though formed in man's image, is a figure of doom.
[Or this:] When she touched a thing, her hands seemed
to take the place of the eye. . . . Her fingers would go
forward, hesitate, tremble, as if they had found a face in
the dark. When her hand finally came to rest, the palm
closed; it was as if she had stopped a crying mouth. . . .[5]

In passages like this, the innermost nerve of a human
being is touched with exquisite marksmanship, a layer of
truth is reached which could not have been attained through
rational description.

But some kind of artistic elucidation occurs not only in
the realm of art proper, where all the transrational faculties of language, magical, metaphorical, musical, can be applied. It can also appear in the rational domain, wherever
a thinker, scholar, or scientist penetrates the jargon of
restrictive research and achieves a presentation of a broader
coherence, a clarification of a comprehensive entity or problem. In all such cases, a congruity of reality and expression,
a rounded form, is accomplished. Often, the attempt to
verbalize a problem, to assemble and connect its various
aspects and ramifications from a transcompartmental van-
tage point, discloses a new range and depth of insight.
It is because of this capacity for verbal clarification, for unfolding in non-specialized language a broad complex of

reality that thinkers like Bergson, Freud, Teilhard de Chardin have been called "artistic."

A well-built sentence whose elements—articulation, meaning, imagery, rhythm—are set in the right proportions, in a balance serving clarity and melos at once and as tightly as possible, is itself a microcosm of closed form. Even in a wordless mathematical demonstration with its "elegant" shortcuts, we may see the perfection of closed form.

Up to this point I have dealt with closed form in its various manifestations: as an integrally finished work, or as embedded in open form, be it through symbolic conformity of two or more levels of existence or by the lucidly synoptic rendering of a character, a situation, a problem, a totality of existence.

It happens, however, that *an open form as such* has artistic validity. There is, apart from organic integrality in the spatial dimensions, still another indispensable property, another *sine qua non* of art, namely, as has been indicated before, its creative extension in the dimension of time, that is, its *evolutional capacity.* Any genuine artistic effort operates on the frontier of the expressible, conquering the hitherto untouched, ungrasped, unrevealed. A work lacking this ultimate effort is stale and without artistic value. Hence novelty, in this sense of initiatory creation, is an essential constituent of a work of art.

Now novelty, of necessity, opens traditionally closed

form, it breaks through the forms which have been established before. Whenever new spheres, new depths of existence are disclosed by a thrust into the unknown, these new experiences will have to be integrated into a further completed whole in order to reach a new and broader, more comprehensive, perfection of form. To be sure, our experience of the fundamental dynamism of reality has shown all closed form to be a mere temporary halt on the road of endlessly moving processes. And yet, lest all efforts be lost in chaotic discontinuity and singularity, new discoveries have to be related with extant realizations; again and again the wholeness of existence must be re-established, a new, wider and more complex wholeness must be apprehended. This is true of the body of our scientific and scholarly knowledge; it is most particularly true of art, whose very principle rests on the creation of form, which means of wholeness.

In this perpetual situation of art between the breaking and the completion of form, it happens that certain experimental ventures, not having reached a settling integration, appear unbalanced, lopsided by the extravagance and overemphasis of their new vistas. They point to a future, still imaginary, supplementation. Open, fragmentary forms that they are, they are nevertheless artistic by virtue of their exploratory quality, their seeking a deeper truth, a congruence with a deeper reality. Take as an example *Tristram Shandy,* that revolutionary work par excellence, which was intentionally created as an open form, to be continued and added to indefinitely, as long as the life of its author would last. Its probes and innovations, disruptive in their time, have been integrated into closed form by the artists of our own epoch.

I have dealt so elaborately with the meaning and the problems of form because I believe them to be crucial not only in regard to art, but in regard to our whole human condition. We live in an era of transition, in which age-old modes of existence, and with them old concepts and structures, are breaking up, while new ones are not as yet clearly recognizable. In such a state of flux—more rapidly moving than ever—in the incessant turmoil of novelty, of discoveries, inventions and experiments, in such a state, concepts like wholeness, like coherence, like history are widely discredited and looked upon with distrust and dis-like. Not only are they felt to be encumbering the freedom of new ventures, they are considered obsolete and invalid. The repudiation of all these concepts implies a discarding of form, for they all—wholeness, coherence, history—are inherent in the concept of form. They all mean and consti-tute *identity*. Indeed, form may be plainly understood as identity. As Richard Blackmur strikingly put it: "Form is the limiting principle by which a thing is itself." Accord-ingly, losing form is equivalent to losing identity.

It is easily understood that wholeness and coherence—

be it rational or transrational coherence—are integral attributes of form and, implicitly, of identity. But, since history is commonly and wrongly seen as an antiquarian past without true relevance to our present life, it has to be expressly stated that history is, in reality, the temporal identity of a live being, a person, a people, the *genus humanum,* and is effective with full force as long as the life of this being lasts.

In all previous transformations of humanity, the breaking up of old forms of existence and conception was immediately linked with the creation of new forms; it was, in fact, partly at least, produced by this creative process. Today, however, the processes of disruption by far outstrip those of new consolidation, indeed the creative processes themselves cannot help producing disjunction. The disjunctive processes appear to have become autonomous. With the various developments which have contributed to this novel state of affairs I will deal later in more detail. At this point I only want to mention one principal factor, and this is the purely functional character of technology which enables it to grow on and on, unimpeded, according to its own self-propelling rationale, and so to outgrow the capacity of human control. "Mechanization takes command," as Siegfried Giedion has proclaimed, it has taken hold of our very existence and of the human mind. Accordingly, any person who still uses organic terms, who raises demands of an organic nature, of a comprehensively *human* nature, who speaks of wholeness, coherence, form, is *eo ipso* considered a romantic reactionary.

Now, matters are not so simple. What I stand and work for, I admit, is what makes human beings human, what keeps humanity, the *genus humanum* human. Unless we want to renounce all care for our essentially human quality, which is ineluctably of an organic nature, we have to cling to the organic concepts with their organic demands and defend them against the onrush of boundless mechanization. It is not wholeness, coherence, form as such that is obsolete. What is obsolete is their inveterate, conventional, static semantics that former generations have left with us. Our task is to re-create, to re-realize these concepts out of our present circumstances. What happens when our avant-gardes try to dispose of them altogether, and how this total abrogation must ultimately lead to atrocities such as we are witnessing today, this I propose to show in the following lectures.

II

The Preliminary Stages
of Disintegration

$\mathcal{I}$N MY first lecture I attempted to establish the nature of form in general and the different modes of artistic form. I tried to determine what it is that makes a work artistic, or better, what it is that induces us to recognize in an intellectual work a quality which we single out as artistic. And it turned out to be always an at least half-conscious effort of a creative person toward the intense rendering of some existential coherence—which is identical with form.

I also stated that in our days, for the first time, such an artistic effort toward the achievement of a new comprehensive form seems lacking. The processes of analytic disjunction prevail over the creative ones, or, to be more correct, they have come to coincide with the creative ones so that, in the main, creation results in disjunction. The following observations will show what a prominent role the influence of science and technology plays in this development.

When we try to reach down to the roots of this disintegrative process, we shall find that, throughout the modern centuries, it pivots on one dominant issue, and this is the complex, paradoxical *relationship between consciousness and the unconscious.* This relationship varied from antagonism to interaction and intertwining; it changed preponderance and exchanged creativity, it started with the supremacy of reason and ended up in the ascendancy of the unconscious and the incapacity of the mind to master its overpopulated, overcreated world—to master it, that means to make it coherent. Consciousness, in point of fact, is awareness of self, awareness of the coherence of the self within a coherence of its surrounding world. And what happened during the last century is a gradual erosion of such awareness. Let me, today, briefly recall the first stages of this process.

Since the late Middle Ages, Christian dogma was increasingly undermined by spreading rationality, and the formerly unquestioned authority of God was taken over by autonomous reason. This meant, on the one hand, what is known as "enlightenment," a secularized continuance of the Christian fight against the sinful body and its dark realm of drives, desires and passions. What had been the accursed work of the Devil, prohibited by divine command, became now a sphere of instinctual error, blind superstition and lack of self-control, to be countered by rational arguments that explained the futility and harmfulness of such indulgence. But by this very means, on the other hand, a

new, conscious attention was directed to this underground
level of the psyche; an alertness was aroused that produced
a first, freely moving empirical psychology. Generally,
however, empirical knowledge was still scarce and supplemented by speculation—only slowly at first the fundamental
methods and instruments of free empirical research were
instituted. The philosophical and scientific systems—there
was hardly a pure, non-speculative science as yet—were
seeking a neatly rational coherence of the secularized universe. Intellectuals did not know such masses of details
as to make them lose their sense of coherence. The absolute
dominance of reason was most strongly felt in the civilizing
subordination of the warring instincts and self-assertion
of the feudal nobility through the etiquette and discipline
of court life, a discipline of elegance, of easy mastery not
only of the body but of the inner life of a person. Sentiments had to be bridled like impetuous horses, curbed to
mere pleasures like nature in the baroque gardens. How far
this discipline went can be gathered from novels like Madame de La Fayette's *Princesse de Clèves* and of Choderlos
de Laclos' *Liaisons dangereuses.* In the playfully controlled,
artfully artistic bearing of this aristocracy, we see the
frightful degenerative extreme of live rational form.

Just as centuries of expanding rationality had finally
shattered the absolute rule of Catholic dogma, so, in like
manner, an underground movement, arising from diverse
sources, brought about during the eighteenth century the

first massive reaction against the dominance of rationalism. We can observe the growth of this oppositional mood in the English and French literature of the period, its increasing emphasis on the irresistible force of passion and sentiment, culminating in Rousseau's attack on civilization; we sense it alive in the incipient malaise of the ruling classes, their weariness with reason that weakened the resistance of the French nobility against the great revolution and made them amenable to its ideas. "Ah reason, reason!" Madame Du Deffand writes to her friend Horace Walpole in 1767, "What is reason? What power does it have? . . . What good can it afford you? It controls passion? This is not true. And if it really were capable of checking the movements of your soul, it would be a hundred times more contrary to your happiness than the passions ever could be. It would mean living so as to sense nothingness, and nothingness, which I take very seriously, is good only inasmuch as we do not sense it." We are on the threshold of romanticism, which extends deep into the nineteenth century, of *Weltschmerz,* of an exaltation of irrationality which throws wide open the gates of the unconscious.

These antecedents of the processes we are concerned with are of course well known, but they are to be kept in mind in considering what follows. From the nineteenth century on, the dialectic between rationality and irrationality, between consciousness in action, which is coherent thinking, and the abrupt impulses of the unconscious, kept accelerat-

ing and growing more complex, more immediate and intense. The antithesis had been fairly clear-cut in the struggle
of reason against passions and emotions. But in the second
half of the eighteenth century a paradoxical intertwining set
in. The volcanic creations of the Storm and Stress movement in Germany, which wanted the boundless forces of
inspiration and ecstasy let loose, were still permeated with
rationalistic argument and witticism. The high-strung emotions of the French Revolution set up a cult of Reason.
And in romanticism, in the philosophical concepts of
Fichte and Hegel, the two elements of the human psyche,
the rational and the irrational, began to interpenetrate to
a degree of near-fusion, when their dialectic was incor-
porated in one evolutional process, and the vital forces
were seen propelling the advance of reason. The astound-
ing insights of Novalis, his far-flung conceptual
combinations, interfused erratic imagination with subtle
rationality. And with such vast extension of vistas went
a broadening and deepening of introspection. Stendhal and
Sénancour, romanticists as they were, thrust far ahead into
modern psychology.

In Stendhal we sense also the influence of the industrial
revolution, which was of even much wider and deeper consequence than the political revolution in France. It radically
changed the whole outlook and the basic values of public
life, not only through its shifting the main concerns of
people from the political to the economic scene, but through

the decisive push it gave to the development of technology and, implicitly of science. It helped to purge the search for knowledge of speculation and to institute a pure-bred empiricism that gradually took hold of all intellectual activity. The initial, very speculative romantic inquiry into the irrational and transrational elements in nature settled down into concrete scientific and artistic studies, into a realistic scrutiny of conditions, which attempted to restrict speculative rationalism, but applied rational methods to empirical search.

Anyway, the rising power of the unconscious was present already in preromantic and romantic irrationalism. Even Goethe, in a conversation with Riemer in 1810, affirmed that "man cannot remain in a state of consciousness very long; he must, again and again, escape into the unconscious, for there lie his roots." Schopenhauer's dominating "will" is a "blind urge," a "dark driving force." And the great German romantic novelist Jean Paul expected stupendous revelations from the exploration of the unconscious, this "inner Africa." These explorations were in full swing in the middle of the nineteenth century. The German psychologist Karl Fortlage, in his *System of Psychology* (1855), went so far as to interpret consciousness as a product of the inhibited unconscious. In literature there had begun to prevail a tendency of seeing the outer world, the world of happenings and action, as a reflection of the inner world of the psyche.

In all these developments, however, consciousness was still in control of the psychic moves, and a rational coherence of events was sought. The so-called psychological novels, *"romans d'analyse,"* of Paul Bourget, for instance, were constructions of model cases, tangles of social, emotional and moral determinants intended to disclose the functioning of psychic life. The motivations of acts and feelings, which authors traced and which the public wanted to know, had to be logically plausible, a character or an act had to be rationally conclusive, to make a story credible and convincing. Moral conflicts and loads of guilt are the intricate agents in Ibsen's meticulously structured psychic dramas.

The revolutionary breakthrough into the realm of the subrational and indeed the subconscious was effected by the great Russian novelists who no longer presented neatly arranged conflicts *in vitro,* but laid bare the true inner life of man with its wild complexity and inconsistency. Moral problems and rational arguments are *some* among other elements in it, they are floating and mingling in the psychic flux, but they do not constitute its principal driving force, and they struggle hard in their effort to assert themselves. The masterful artistry of these authors was capable of holding that vast turmoil of motifs and motivations together.

Since this turn of the tide—a real caesura in intellectual history—people gradually came to understand that psychic

life does not proceed in a rationally orderly manner of evident causality, but rather by way of very different, much
more dense and intense linkings of often flashy immedi-
acy, connections whose "reasons" extend into such vital
depths that they are rationally inaccessible and can hardly
be expressed in logical sequence. Associations emerge between apparently quite remote fields, somewhat like electri-
cal contacts; paradoxical relations loom between rational
opposites. And in the rendering of such instantaneous
sparking, an ultimate human truth suddenly flares up.

Contemporaneously with the Russian authors, a man, a
live receptacle of such occurrences, appeared in Germany,
endowed with a faculty of subtlest expression. The most
artistic among modern philosophers, Friedrich Nietzsche, a
multifaceted genius, pre-sensed all the centrifugal tendencies of our time, destructive as they are and at the same
time creative: He comprehended in his mind the most contradictory trends. He, who himself perished by the bursting
of an overtaxed, overexerted consciousness, stated propheti-
cally that "the growing consciousness is a danger and a
disease."

What followed in our own century was this: From its
early beginnings the unconscious moved into the center of
attention; it became the object of scientific and artistic
scrutiny. The first systematic study of this realm of the
psyche, psychoanalysis, was instituted by Sigmund Freud,
shortly after William James had spotted "fringes" and

"gaps" of consciousness. The scientific advance was accompanied by new novelistic techniques of probing into the psychic underground: stream of consciousness, free association, inner monologue. Phenomenal reality, pervaded as it is by rationality, was felt to be a fictitious surface reality, and in the course of investigation true reality was seen to recede to ever deeper subliminal levels until it appeared quite unfathomable.

Finally, in the cataclysms of the world wars, and under the stress of an autonomous proliferation of technology and the crowding of events, developments and populations that went with it, there occurred the actual breakdown of rational control. The overstrained capacity for maintaining a sensible coherence of events, which means true consciousness, yielded and turned into anarchic confusion and the unleashing of the most savage drives.

Nathalie Sarraute describes the mental process in her essay *De Dostoiewski à Kafka*: "The time has passed," she writes, "when Proust could venture to believe that 'by pushing his impression to that ultimate limit of penetration (he could) attempt to reach that ultimate bottom where the truth, the real universe and our authentic impression rest.' After all, informed by successive delusions, everybody was well aware that there was no ultimate ground. 'Our authentic impression' had been revealed to consist of multifold layers of depth, and these depths extended *ad infinitum*. The depth that Proust's analysis had uncovered,

[35]

turned out to be just another surface. The still deeper depth that the inner monologue, on which so legitimate hopes were placed, had brought to light, proved a surface again. And the immense leap of psychoanalysis, sweeping all stages and traversing several levels of depth in one stride, had shown the inefficacy of classical introspection, and makes us question the absolute value of all methods of research. So, the *homo absurdus* was the dove of the ark, the messenger of deliverance."[1]

Nathalie Sarraute disregards the fact that each of these thrusts into the psychic underground has conquered for our consciousness a stage of reality and has brought to light a level of being that has its lasting place in the expanse of existence. Existence, to be sure, is bottomless, it reaches into unfathomable grounds of emergence. But this in no way nullifies the reality and validity of the various gradations of psychic depth, as apprehended by artistic and scientific explorations. Something irrevocable happened through these explorations: they vastly extended the field of consciousness, whether we could control it or not.

A related process is apparent in the visual arts. The portraits of Van Gogh, of Kokoschka, of Beckmann no longer render the immediate, physiognomical appearance of a person—this the masters of the Renaissance and since have already exhausted. Their vision reaches beyond these surfaces; they seek "for the bridge from the visible to the invisible," as Beckmann put it, for the psychic aura of a human being. Even the landscapes of these artists expose, animistically as it were, a psychic quality of the sceneries. In further pursuits artists were led to explore the structures of phenomenality as such, spatial forms as such, and thereby the analytical decomposition of the world of objects. The counterpart of the *homo absurdus* in literature may be seen in certain surrealist creations.

The literature of the absurd developed, out of an age-old genre, a new form which, by lifting the human scene to an imaginary level, allowed a sublimation and concentration of the perplexities of our condition. This new form is the *parable*. In a most genuine and accomplished style it was inaugurated, of course, by Kafka, but used by a long line of authors from Sartre, Camus, Ernst Jünger to Beckett, Genet, Ionesco and many others to this very day.

But at the same time the growing ascendancy of the unconscious brought about a turn of utmost importance. The unconscious no longer remained a mere *object* of conscious acts of exploration; it seized upon the artistic *act itself* and emerged as the very *enactor* of artistic creation, as we see happen in "beat" literature and action painting. Let us follow this turn a little more closely to see where it leads and what it implies.

Any artistic work, to be sure, has its ultimate roots in the unconscious. In creating his work, the artist always moves partly in his psychic underground; and even in the most strained efforts of artistic consciousness a residue of

[37]

unconscious process inheres. No artist has ever been able fully to comprehend and control the scope of his work. After its completion the work starts on a life of its own, and only then it unfolds its whole meaning and consequence, unknown by its author. Picasso has stressed the role of the unconscious in his work. "When I paint," he said, "my objective is to show what I have found, not what I was looking for. In art, intentions are not sufficient. . . . I go for a walk in the forest of Fontainebleau. I get 'green' indigestion. I must get rid of this sensation into a picture. . . . A painter paints to unload himself of feelings and visions. . . ."[2] Similarly, Kafka, in his conversations with Gustav Janouch, said that his story, *The Stoker,* was the reminiscence of a dream, and that *The Judgment* was a nightmare which had to be recorded, "stated" as a measure of defense and protection. "One pictures things in order to banish them. My stories are a manner of closing the eyes." And further on he states: "The dream reveals a reality that our imagination cannot reach. Hence the terrifying quality of life—the heartrending quality of art."[3] These sentences afford a clue to Kafka's entire work.

Both these artists, however, have given the greatest conscious care to the form of conveying their experiences. Such scrupulous control, the effect of a long-trained meditative sensibility, is apparent in their creations; it is also explicitly attested. Picasso tell us of his proceeding, which he calls "a sum of destructions," but which actually is true abstraction,

[38]

as exemplified by that sequence of drawings in which he gradually divested the figure of a bull of its naturalistic detail until the very essence of its structure lay bare. "I do a picture," Picasso says, "—then I destroy it. . . . It would be very interesting to preserve photographically . . . the metamorphoses of a picture. Possibly, one might discover the path followed by the brain in materializing a dream. . . . *You must always start with something* [emphasis mine]. Afterwards you can remove all traces of reality. There's no danger then, anyway, because the idea of the object will have left an indelible mark. It is what started the artist off, excited his ideas and stirred up his emotions. Ideas and emotions will in the end be prisoners in his work."[4] Kafka's diaries give evidence of his constant struggle for utmost precision in describing a phenomenon, of the "frightful strain and joy"—almost the same words as Flaubert's—to feel "how the story developed before me, how I moved ahead in troubled waters. Several times during this night [when he wrote *The Judgment*] I bore my weight on my back." This is what distinguishes the true poet: writing, he has to bear his whole weight, the weight of his life, on his back.

So these great artists are fully aware of the unconscious sources of their creation: they consciously include the unconscious, they acknowledge the part it plays, in their creation; yet they guide it and work it out.

In the products of tachism, of action painting, of "beat"

literature, and of a certain phase of multiform dadaism, however, the unconscious is unleashed as sheer raw material; it is released intentionally, programmatically. In this way a peculiar, inorganic conjunction of consciousness and the unconscious takes place; what John Cage, in regard of music, explicitly recommends: a purposeful purposelessness.

In painting, it began with the revolt against the frame —that last buttress of form. (The impressionists, even before, had cut off segments of the thematic "objective" text of paintings—parts of figures, objects, scenery—in favor of purely pictorial concordance.) But the action painters' concern is no longer the finished work so much as the *act* of painting, which is supposed to guide the painter in his quest for personal identity. Mark Rothko, who is not precisely an action painter, still declared that "a painting is not a picture of an experience; it is an experience."[5] And a disciple of Rothko's, Okada, prescribed explicitly: *"start painting with nothing and let it grow"* [emphasis mine].

Action painters are distrustful of the control of consciousness, they stand *in* the developing picture and let themselves be determined by an unguided spontaneous incentive. "When I am in my painting," Jackson Pollock said, "I'm not aware of what I'm doing. It is only after a sort of 'get acquainted' period that I see what I have been about . . . the painting has a life of its own. I try to let it come through. . . . When you're painting out of your unconscious, figures are bound to emerge. . . . Something in me knows where I am going and—well, painting is a state of being." And Franz Kline affirmed that "it's free association from the start to the finished state."

Edward Albee in describing his creative process uses almost the same words as Jackson Pollock. His proceeding amounts to what could be called "action writing." "When I was writing *Tiny Alice*," Albee declared in an interview, "to a certain extent, I didn't have any idea what I was doing. When I write plays, the writing of the play is an act of discovery for me. I find out what was bothering me. And a certain time after the play, I can say to myself, 'Ha! that is what I intended.' "

The results of the painting acts of action painting and of the "New York School" are those whole walls of aggressive line and color whirls, full of ebullient vitality, or "monochrome" paintings, or shaded color squares, divided by horizontal or vertical lines. The effects on devotees consist, as Rothko once indicated, in a kind of mystical communication and ecstasy, similar to those aroused by the *musique concrète* and the frameless, static dynamism of hot jazz.

Such displays of the unconscious are, however, often supplemented by efforts of consciousness, that is, commentaries, interpretations, titles which are affixed to the exhibited paintings. Indeed, with some of these painters such interpretations appear retroactively as original intentions revealed by the creative process. The exposition of an apparently accidental arrangement is sometimes presented as "abstraction."

True abstraction is brought about by an act of concentrating a phenomenon, a process, an impression, an argument to a point where their essence is laid bare. In abstract expressionism, however, nothing is recognizable from which these products may have been abstracted. They lack a substratum of abstraction and accordingly also that trace of creative effort that can be felt in any former work of art or of thought, be it ever so accomplished, in itself.

So what produces such paintings is not abstraction, but rather reduction. "Minimalism" is the explicit slogan. To be sure, reduction can also be seen as a kind of abstraction, an inverse abstraction, an abstraction into the total concreteness of bare material, a divestment of substance.

A paradigm of total reduction may be seen in Ad Reinhardt's huge canvas, which he called *Abstract Painting* and in which he took enormous pains to eliminate all traces of any, even non-objective, substratum; nothing is left but the bare material of paint. He described it as follows:

> A square (neutral, shapeless) canvas, five feet wide, five feet high, as high as a man, as wide as a man's outstretched arms (not large, not small, sizeless), trisected (no composition) one horizontal form negating one vertical form (formless, no top, no bottom, directionless), three (more or less) dark (lightless), non-contrasting (colorless) colors, brushwork brushed out to remove

[42]

brushwork, a mat, flat, free-hand painted surface (gloss-less, textureless, non-linear, no hard edge, no soft edge) which does not reflect its surroundings—a pure, abstract, non-objective, timeless, spaceless, changeless, relationless, disinterested painting—an object that is self-conscious (no unconsciousness), ideal, transcendent, aware of nothing but art (absolutely no anti-art).

No inkling is given as to what is meant by "art." Art seems to be a process of voiding, a *tour de force* of reaching the absolute zero-point.

Many "abstract" painters still feel compelled to attribute to their works some extrapictorial, metaphysical substance. But that pictorial reduction, that "abstraction" into the material elements of painting, leads straight to "pop art," the abandonment not only of all pictorial substance, but of painting altogether, which means the display of material objects as such, or better, of fragments of objects, or objects as fragments, of our overcrowded and disrupted world. We shall presently encounter another, convergent motive force leading to pop art.

Such fragments of our present world, however, are brought into extraneous interrelation, indeed sometimes into an exquisite formal balance by an artistic consciousness as we find at work in certain collages and assemblages—in a way reminiscent of Gottfried Benn's poetry. They render the coexistence of the wildly contrasting residues of our daily life, relics of nature with pieces of technology, the closely familiar with the oddly rotten. Hovering over them one senses a mood of melancholy irony, of aimless rebellion, such as it is vocalized in the manifestations of the "beat" movement.

The "beat" movement follows Allen Ginsberg's call: "Unscrew the locks from the doors! Unscrew the doors themselves from their jambs!"[6] Here again, emotions, impressions, day- and night-dreams, and scraps of knowledge are let loose in rapturous medley. Ginsberg's and Kerouac's master, William Burroughs, declares: "I write about what is in front of my senses at the moment of writing. I do not presume to impose 'story' or 'plot' or 'continuity.' "[7] But again, contrasts are deliberately sharpened.

The deep disappointment—an erroneous disappointment —about the bottomlessness of the unconscious, as voiced by Nathalie Sarraute, contributed not only to the emergence of the *homo absurdus*. Still another conclusion was drawn from the experience of existential insecurity, again by Nathalie Sarraute. "Modern man," she says, "body without soul, tossed about by hostile forces, was ultimately nothing else but what he appeared from outside."[8] The despair of gaining a firm stand in the unconscious and of casting an anchor in the immense chaos of our world had its share in turning artists back to the presentation of the crudest surfaces of things, to pure, immediate materiality. "It looks," Hans Richter, a former Dadaist, writes, "as if people today needed the instantly palpable material object to hold on to as a confirmation of their presence in the

[44]

world; as if man could find himself substantiated only through his contact with his five senses, since in him all is broken up and uncertain. An inner void seems to force him outward, an urge to convince him of his existence by way of the object, because the subject, man himself, got lost. . . . Our generation has become so greedy of presence that even the lid of a W.C. is holy to us, we are not satisfied with seeing it pictured, we want to *have* it altogether, bodily."[9]

The pop artist Jim Dine, who exhibits "self-portraits" in the shape of empty bathrobes, surrounded by tools and other objects, told an interviewer that having seen an advertisement of a bathrobe in the *New York Times,* he first intended to use it at will when it suddenly looked to him as if he himself were in it. We find a striking correspondence to this notion in the French *nouveau roman,* wrongly characterized as *"neo-realism."* In the novels of Robbe-Grillet, man is left vacant amidst his prevailing surroundings; he appears as a hollow, ghost-like existence in situations he is not seen attending, or he is merely functionally reflected in surreally protrusive objects and behavioral responses. In the novel *Jalousie,* the husband is reduced to a constantly present watchful look which in reality should emanate from a strong emotion, but which, on principle, has to be kept completely impersonal. Milieus, incidents, moves are pictured in most finicky detail, which no look could ever absorb, not even a clinically disinterested one, let alone one that is passionately involved. The story, which takes place on a tropical estate, consists of a monologue of observation, sustained throughout the book by the unidentified husband who suspects his wife of a clandestine relation with a daily dinner guest. The house, the scenery, the plantations with their workers, the service, the drinks, the eating habits and insignificant conversations of the suspected couple, the repeated crushing of centipedes, all this is described most meticulously, indeed sometimes statistically, by the watching eye. Let me give you a brief example:

A . . . [the wife, unnamed, just an initial] is standing on the veranda, at the corner of the house, near the square column that supports the southwest corner of the roof. She is leaning both hands on the railings, facing south, looking over the garden and the whole valley. / She is in full sunlight. The sun strikes her directly on the forehead. But she does not mind it, even at noon. Her foreshortened shadow falls perpendicularly across the flagstones, of which it covers, lengthwise, no more than one. A quarter of an inch behind it begins the roof shadow, parallel with the railing. The sun is almost at its zenith. / The two extended arms are an equal distance from either side of the hips. The hands are both holding the wooden handrail in the same way. Since A . . . is standing with half her weight on each of her high-heeled shoes, the symmetry of the whole body is perfect./A . . . is standing in front of the living-room, directly opposite the dirt road that comes down from the highway. Through the glass she looks straight ahead of her, toward the place where the road enters the dusty courtyard, which the shadow of the house darkens with a strip about three yards wide. The rest of the courtyard is white in the sunlight. / The large room, in comparison, seems dark. Her dress takes on a cold blue tinge from the shadows. A . . . does not move. She continues to stare at the courtyard and the road between the banana trees, straight ahead of her.[10]

There is not the slightest hint of any sentiment, of tenderness, of longing or anger, hardly even of emotion among the suspected couple. I must say, if the husband is really to be identified with his pedantic eye, it is more than understandable that the woman has an affair with another man.

The theory of this school, which I would rather call *presentism,* is explained by Robbe-Grillet as follows:

Instead of [the] universe of "signification" . . . we must try . . . to construct a world both more solid and more immediate. Let it be first of all by their presence that objects and gestures establish themselves, and let this presence continue to prevail over whatever explanatory theory may try to enclose them in a system of references, whether emotional, sociological, Freudian, or metaphysical. In this future universe of the novel, gestures and objects will be there before being something; and they will still be there afterwards, hard, unalterable, eternally present, mocking their own "meaning," that meaning which vainly tries to reduce them to the role of precarious tools, of a temporary and shameful fabric woven exclusively—and deliberately —by the superior human truth expressed in it. . . . Henceforth . . . novels will gradually lose their instability and their secrets, will renounce . . . that suspect interiority which Roland Barthes has called "the romantic heart of things" . . . not only do we no longer consider the world as our own, our private property, designed according to our needs . . . but we no longer even believe in its "depth."[11]

It seems not to have occurred to Robbe-Grillet that the universe closely surrounding our life consists predominantly and increasingly of man-made objects, objects constructed for human purposes. Pure nature is gradually receding into the cosmic spheres; objects and beings that are genuinely independent of man give way to artifacts in which human "significances," human conditions and changes are indelibly contained, and which certainly will not be there afterwards any more than they have been there before the emergence of man. On the contrary, they prove more transitory, more temporary than even man himself. This whole transformation of our surroundings and circumstances, this externalization of our life and the concomitant loss of depth, expressed in the *nouveau roman* itself and in Robbe-Grillet's theory in particular, means something indeed; it indicates something more than its surface presence, namely a transformation of man himself, his transition from individual to collective existence.

The new novelists' radical attention to sheer materiality involves, however, its very reversal. The subtly constructed works of Robbe-Grillet show the inherent connection of the extreme of quasi-tactual phenomenalism with the opposite extreme of acutest abstractness, the turn of one extreme into the other. The completely objectified rendition of a world more and more externalized, and the total elimination of human sentiment, this is an artistic proceeding of utmost reduction. It can be undertaken only by means of the keenest analytical pursuance of a factuality that is unreal in its actually imperceptible minutiae. The flow of actuality is dissected into slightest particulars. It leads to a formalism, a skeletal form in which all vital substance has faded away. A ghostly consciousness is confronted with itself.

To be sure, these creations present a consciously built coherence and insofar, they are accomplished form. But in spite of its fine intense formulations, this is a form that comes close to sheer construction. For the divorce of the sphere of action from psychic reaction, the elimination of human sentiment, of human significance, and of the sensitively registered part of happenings, makes them humanly incomplete. Indeed it indicates a specific, very frightening mode and degree of disintegration, with which I am going to deal in the next lecture, when we come to consider the jeopardy of artistic language, indeed of all language as a means of human communication in our times.

THE PRELIMINARY STAGES OF DISINTEGRATION

Illustrations

Picasso: Six Stages of Abstraction
Abstract Expressionism and the New York School
Assemblage
Pop Art
Op Art

Pablo Picasso, "Abstractions of a Bull" (Six Lithographs)

Collection of Mrs. Meric Callery
Photo: Soichi Sunami

Jackson Pollock, "Number 8" (1950)

Collection of Mrs. Enid A. Haupt
Photo: Soichi Sunami

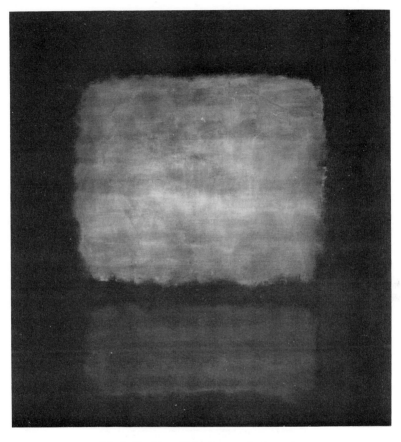

Mark Rothko, "Number 19" (1958)
Collection, The Museum of Modern Art, New York
Photo: Oliver Baker

Barnett Newman, "Abraham" (1949)
Collection, The Museum of Modern Art, New York
Photo: Soichi Sunami

Ad Reinhardt, "Abstract Painting" (1960–61)
Collection, The Museum of Modern Art, New York
Photo: R. Peter Petersen

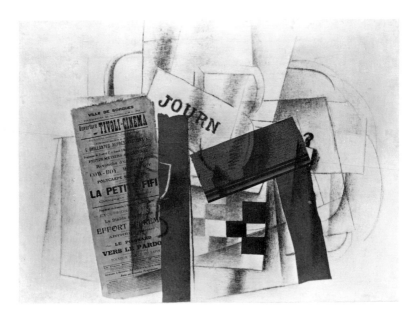

Georges Braque, "The Program" (1913)

Collection, Mr. and Mrs. Bernard J. Reis
Photo: Soichi Sunami

Kurt Schwitters, "Cherry Picture" (1921)

Collection, The Museum of Modern Art, New York
Mr. and Mrs. A. Atwater Kent, Jr. Fund
Photo: Soichi Sunami

Joan Miró, "Poetic Object" (1936)

Collection, The Museum of Modern Art, New York
Gift of Mr. and Mrs. Pierre Matisse
Photo: Soichi Sunami

Louise Nevelson, "Royal Tide I" (1960)

Collection, The Martha Jackson Gallery, New York
Photo: Rudolph Burckhardt

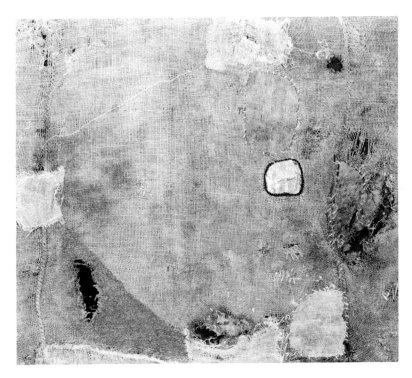

Alberto Burri, "Composition 8" (1953)
Collection, The Museum of Modern Art, New York
Mr. and Mrs. David M. Solinger Fund
Photo: Soichi Sunami

Jasper Johns, "Flashlight" (1960)

Collection, Ferus Gallery, Los Angeles (Mr. Irving Blum)
Photo: Ileana Sonnabend, Paris

Armand Arman, "Glug-Glug" (1961)
Collection, Galleria Schwarz, Milan
Photo: Bacci

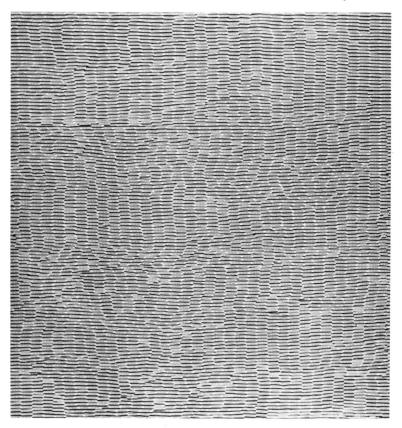

Yayoi Kusama, "Air Mail Stickers" (1962)
Collection, Whitney Museum of American Art
Gift of Hanford Yang
Photo: Oliver Baker

Nobuaki Kojima, Figure (untitled, 1964)

Collection, Mr. William S. Lieberman, New York

George Segal, "Couple on a Bed" (1965)
Collection Sidney Janis Gallery, New York

Tadasky, "A-101" (1964)
Collection, The Museum of Modern Art, New York
Larry Aldrich Foundation Fund

JN THE preceding lecture I surveyed the antecedents and the first stages of the disintegration of artistic form. Let me recall these stages. The first symptoms, in the eighteenth century, were a weariness of rational discipline among the ruling nobility and intelligentsia and an increasing emphasis on the irrational forces of the psyche. As a result, the unconscious became a predominant *object* of artistic and scientific exploration until it finally seized upon the *act* of artistic performance and emerged as the very *enactor* of the creative process. This involved a dissolution of rational and, subsequently, even of transrational coherence. The disillusioning experience of the ultimately unfathomable depth of the unconscious, and of the unmasterable, labyrinthian condition of people's life and environment caused their minds to revert to the surface level of existence: sheer present and presence, to the immediately palpable sensory appearance of objects and gestures. Hence, the behavioristic

[73]

approach to the phenomena of psychic and social life. Hence, the turn to pop art and the radical elimination of human sentiment and motivation from narrative in the *nouveau roman*. All this implies a crippling of vital coherence.

We have now to consider another most important agent of the disintegrative process: the *growing insecurity of language and human communication*.

The problematic nature of language and implicitly the uncertainty of human communication has troubled people's minds for more than two and a half centuries. The awareness of it dawns in Locke's inquiry into the "imperfection of Words"; it manifests itself in *Tristram Shandy* and in *The Sorrows of Young Werther*. It grew with the increasing complexity of Western man's life and psychic condition, and more rapidly with the expansion of the collectivizing, instrumentalizing, functionalizing apparatus of our daily subsistence, which drives a wedge between man and man, silencing, atrophying the expression of inner life and thus severing inner truth from compelling actuality.

The scrutiny of language issued from different sources: literary, philosophical, and, last but not least, psychological. It developed into a widespread process, in which the various trends and effects interact. In the domain of letters it brought art to question itself, its own function, methods, capacity of expression, and, in a more advanced stage of the process, this inquiry into the communicative medium

[74]

merged with the substance to be conveyed: experimental techniques prevail over and finally become the very subject matter of works of art. In true art, as it was said before, "form" and "content" are only two aspects of one and the same thing: the what determines the how. Recently, however, the order is reversed: the how not only determines, it downright constitutes the what. It is no accident that in our days a concept and a slogan was so persuasively raised, proclaiming that the medium is the message.

This development starts from the poetic incentive of Mallarmé, whose innovation appears as the ultimate source of recent linguistic experiments. What actuated Mallarmé's principle was, above all, a reaction against the preceding styles—for a full understanding of a literary movement it is always necessary to consider its epochal position and opposition. The French *poésie pure* arose from repugnance against the time-worn "philosophical" poetry of romanticism and classicism as well as against the unpoetic, descriptive aim of naturalism, hence against ideas or facts as poetic motives and motifs. The new poets' weariness of a mode of expression made hollow by sentimentality and rhetoric drew their creative attention to the body of language, to the self-contained effects of words. "The work of art in its complete purity," Mallarmé writes, "implies the disappearance of the poet's oratorical presence. The poet leaves the initiative to the words, to the clash of their mobilized diversities. The words ignite through mutual reflexes like

[75]

a flash of fire over jewels. Such reflexes replace that respiration [of the poet] perceptible in the old lyrical aspiration or the enthusiastic personal direction of the sentence."[1] This assertion shows clearly the turn against the previous declamatory style which was still prevalent at the time. Even more revealing is another statement intended to avert possible misunderstandings. "I do not see," Mallarmé declares, "—and this is my intense opinion—that anything that was beautiful in the past could ever become extinct. I remain convinced that in most cases the grand tradition . . . will always be followed. But, to be sure, this will be achieved only if the venerable echoes are not disturbed for the sake of a puff of sentimentality, or for the sake of a narrative. Every soul is a melody that has to be revivified ever anew, and this is what everyone's flute or fiddle is for."[2] Just as Flaubert wanted the novel to be strictly objective, and rejected any personal intervention by the author, so, correspondingly, Mallarmé insisted that the "enthusiastic" poet disappear from the finished poem. Yet in his poems Mallarmé never gave up the coherence of meaning and the poet's control.

Mallarmé's suggestion was realized by Joyce in *Finnegans Wake,* but in a very different sense. With him, the ignition of words through confrontation has given way to their *quasi-autonomous* association through sounds, producing a concentration of meanings.

It was Dadaism which actually came to practice a completely free, undirected assemblage of words and linguistic

[76]

sounds. This had been preluded by Rimbaud, for whom, however, this was plainly jocose nonsense (*connerie*), by Mallarmé's metaphysical idea of chance as the origin of things (in the *Coup de dés*), also by Futurist ventures (particularly Marinetti's), and by Apollinaire's principle of coincidence. Dada, this exuberantly inventive movement, uncommitted, flexible, humorous as it was, using all imaginable means of provocation, anticipated everything that today is carried on by pedantic bores. In Dada we still sense the prime freshness of militant protest, and behind it the groping for a new order. Richard Huelsenbeck, one of the founders of the movement in 1916, described their common motivation as follows: "The Dadaists—far ahead of their time—were people whose peculiar sensibility made them aware of the approaching chaos and who tried to overcome it. . . . [They] were creative irrationalists who understood (unconsciously rather than consciously) what the chaos signified . . . they loved the non-sensical without, however, losing sight of the sensible."[3] For them the nonsense remained nonsense.

In the meantime chaos has fully erupted. The "beat" poets, while still revolting, seem to have settled down in it, and indeed to overstress it. In the poetry of Ginsberg, Gregory Corso, and others of the movement, the boundless rhapsodizing of Walt Whitman, reversed into disillusionment by the experiences of our age, is kept in motion through psychic, visual, and verbal free association.

[77]

Thus, since the end of the nineteenth century and increasingly since the beginning of our century, the literary development shows a growing tendency toward dissolution of the linguistic form. Syntactic and rational coherence is broken up, construction gives way to contraction or fragmentation. Yet, in all the works we have considered so far, language still remains human discourse. Human beings speak to human beings, be it to themselves.

Now, however, among the most recent intellectual generations, under the objectifying and functionalizing influence of science and technology, something radically new has been undertaken: *Language has been divorced from its human source.* With the present avant-grade movements, spreading all over the countries and continents of the West, language has ceased to be human communication. Just as the objects crowding around us are no longer implements of man, but are given by subservient man an autonomous, overbearing character, so language is treated as an external independent object, detached from its human manifestation and meaning. This does not prevent its free intellectual manipulation; on the contrary, it makes it all the more possible. The isolation of words from their significative coherence, which started as early as 1912 with Marinetti's concept of "free words" (*parole in libertà*), is equivalent to its severance from its substance, which is human feelings, thoughts, and conceptions; what remains is a devised free association of linguals, or a promiscuity of fractured, de-

funct meanings, corpses of meaning. The inanimate word
has nothing left to keep it from further disintegration into
its components, into syllables and letters; indeed the letters
themselves do not subsist any longer as form units, they
break asunder into parts of their linear figurations, and
what started as poetry ends up in typography. It thereby
passes over into the sphere of the visual arts, where the
wordless and so also the wordlessly transobjective is
legitimate: matters beyond verbal expressibility, subtle
balances, proportions, spatial forms, indeed most delicate
psychic messages find here their accomplished expression
—as originally with Mondrian, Klee, Braque, Miró, Arp,
among others, and recently, to quote only a few examples,
with Nicholson, Manessier, Vieira da Silva, Gabo, Bissier.
In the end, the alphabetical leavings of post-lettristic writers
meet with the imaginative letter paraphrases of artists like
Klee, Mark Tobey, Tomlin, Ben Shahn, Steinberg, which
derive from what Tobey called "the calligraphic impulse."

This is the process we are witnessing. It evidently corresponds to the developments leading to pop art—and op
art in its stereotypically reductive and repetitive variety*—

* What I describe is the growing prevalence of a general evolutional
tendency. Of course, artistic ingenuity does not become extinct with
the advent of even the most precarious fashion of presentation. Indeed
the artistic imagination continues to be stimulated into probing fresh
means of exertion opened up by a new trend. So even among the products of pop art, and most particularly of op art, with its craft deriva-
tions and new dynamic extensions, we encounter along with plain
hamburgers and dull geometrical stereotypes, combinations and inventions of a delightful quality.

and to "punctual," "concrete," and unintegrated electronic music. Indeed, since Futurism, the borderlines between the various arts have become fluid.

The same uncertainty about human communication, the same distrust of the language of meanings can be found in the attempts of analytical and linguistic logic to establish most rigorous delimitations of conceptual terms, efforts that produce even more dissection and paralyzing insecurity. The heroic struggle of that prodigious, but dangerous genius, Wittgenstein, to rid us of problems ended up in unanswerable questions. All these contemporary endeavors are pervaded by a longing for the safety of the mathematical formula, which, however, can warrant such safety only when applied to models, theoretical and mechanical constructions, or statically circumscribed physical areas, but will never be able fully to comprehend the dynamically variable conditions of human existence.

The avant-garde movement has taken hold of all artistic domains. Under the fanfares of thrilling innovations sounding everywhere, from Brazil to Iceland, literature fades away, not only into graphics, but into motley sound associations and mechanistic regimentation. There are "pop poems," "audiopoems," "machine poems," "concrete," "visual" and "phonic" poetry. Henri Chopin's "audiopoem" is a flux of natural and mechanical sounds (spoken and recorded by the poet) ranging from breathings, grunts, clicks, and whistles, to dentist's drills, circular saws, ship's horns, and distant planes. Inasmuch as this performance is meant to be accompanied by a simultaneous show of illustrative drawings, as projected by Henri Garnier, it is an example of what is proclaimed as "spatial poetry," connecting phonetic and visual dimensions. We have poetic ventures called "topographies," "articulations," "combinations," "constellations," "demonstrations," "paralinguistic modes of communication," "permutational art." We have the "electrolyrics" of the Portuguese school, the lettristic "mecha-aesthetics, integral and infinitesimal," we have Max Bense's "programming of beauty," characterized as "precise pleasures."

Many people, including intellectuals, are inclined to consider these movements as vogues of folly that will pass. But it seems to me that they are to be taken very seriously. They are the outcome of an evolutional trend, a consistent artistic and broadly human development. The overwhelming preponderance of collectivity with its scientific, technological and economic machinery, the daily flow of new discoveries and inventions that perpetually change aspects and habits of thought and practice, the increasing incapacity of individual consciousness to cope with the abstract anarchy of its environment, and its surrender to a collective consciousness that operates anonymously and diffusely in our social and intellectual institutions—all this has shifted the center of gravity of our world from existential to func-

[81]

tional, instrumental, and mechanical ways of life. At the same time the hypertrophy of functional rationalization has produced an overcompensating irrationality, reversing to the bodily concrete or spiraling to the absurd. Hence the products of the avant-gardes display a strange blend of erratic imaginative vagaries with technological and pseudo-scientific aspirations. Fragments of unconscious and sensory experience are in a ghostly manner treated with an ex-actitude derived from rational consciousness and informa-tion.

Let us look a little closer into the arguments, programs, and experimental practices of the recent language opera-tors.

We are faced with the basic question: what is language? what is it for?

No human time is known to us when language was any-thing other than a more or less articulate mode of expres-sion of the human being, expression of human feelings, experiences, thoughts, aims and desires. We shall never be able to trace the actual genesis of human language, but there can hardly be any doubt that it was the urge to express and to communicate, one passing into the other, which brought language forth. Today, for the first time in history, language is being divorced from its human source and treated as a separate, independent thing.

Among the linguistic experiments of the avant-gardes *three trends and stages* are distinguishable, although they are mingled and blurred in the process. There is much enthusiastic confusion. What all of them have in common is the isolation of linguistic material, which means getting rid of what is seen as content. The movement started with the elimination of sentiment—a tendency which we found previously in the *nouveau roman*—elimination of all "emotional encumbrances," which are said to "deform and misuse the words." The word is supposed to constitute pure information, "whose meaning is disclosed through the constellation,* that is, the experimental combination with other words." The aim is "getting behind the mirror" (*attraversare lo specchio*) as one of the Italian innovators, Alfredo Giuliani, puts it, the "mirror" being human expression. "There exist," he declares, "certain modes of that mechanical esperanto of imagination . . . which in themselves cannot be considered negative or positive, but simply factual; they form part of the material of that 'heteronomous semanticity' which the epoch offers to the writer. . . . It is . . . archaic to attempt using a contemplative language, which pretends to preserve, not so much the value and the possibility of contemplation, but its unreal syntax."[4] According to Giuliani, imagination itself in our days is discontinuous, "schizomorphic," and calls for "asyntactism."[5]

---

* "By constellation I understand the arrangement of a few, diverse words, in such a way that their mutual relationship does not come about primarily through syntactical means, but through their material, concrete co-presence in the same compass." Eugen Gomringer, *Material T,* Darmstadt, 1958.

A German experimentator, Helmut Heissenbüttel, is more explicit. He contends that the old "withered" syntactical model, subject-object-predicate, is obsolete and no longer capable of conveying the new, the not-yet-graspable that is forming in our age. He wants to "penetrate into the innermost of language, to break it up and to sound out its remotest, most concealed relationships."[6]

Since the word combination of a regular, syntactic sentence is formed to express something human, a substratum deriving from a human source and "encumbered" by uncontrollable personal overtones—by sentiments, sensibilities, experiences, and contemplations—only combinations of words, originally incoherent among each other, must appear capable of warding off such interferences. But, apart from the unescapable fact that even single words carry, indeed consist of nothing else than fragmented residues of some human significance, it is hardly conceivable how such combinations of incoherent sense-fragments could ever establish meaningful information. And where is "the new, the not-yet-graspable" to be registered, if not in the human mind? From where can we expect a new language to issue if not from an extreme human effort to form an expression of new experience?

This perverted "information theory" leads up—or rather down, as we shall see—to the *second* stage of the avant-garde movement, which may be seen in the theses of another German writer, Franz Mon. "The language of instantaneous composition [that is, composition disregarding communicative meaning]," he writes, "is achieved through purely physiological articulation, in contrast to the language of communication. . . . In the former, it is possible to reduce the meaning-values to such an extent that the articulatory process itself becomes a sign of intrinsic gesticulatory value, whereas the articulatory process disappears in communication. In instantaneous composition, the next step follows spontaneously from the constellation immediately preceding. The organs of articulation move of themselves from one position to the next."[7] This is further explained in another statement:

> Immediately at the threshold of articulation, noticeable in the particular chewing motion of the speech organs, lie the elementary words (*Kernworte*), which, this side of imagery already penetrate under our skin; in them erotic and pre-erotic elementals are quite concrete; words are stimulatory forms of a reality that we often can reach only with their help. . . . Speaking, right at the threshold of articulation, is dance of the lips, the tongue, the teeth, articulated, and therefore accurate motion; words, the basic figures of the dance, carry along with them, to be sure, meanings, relations, shadows of images, but slurred into a distinctive motion, that is, directed solely by itself. . . . Long before all speech, lips, tongue, and teeth have performed the movements of appropriation, destruction, love and lust, they are informed by these experiences when they begin to form for speaking. Inevitably, the gestures of speaking will blend with the traits of those elementary movements . . . to this end, they avail them-

[85]

selves of the most fleeting stuff, the air, squeezing, pushing, sucking it to probe the elementary gestics the world abounds with. Here, we are dog, pig, bull, and rooster. . . .[8]

In this interesting concept, the attempt to reach beyond the language of meanings takes us to a prehuman, animal level, to a sphere below an unconscious—since the unconscious presupposes consciousness—a sphere also below imagery, a sphere where language consists of gestures— gestures *before,* not, as Richard Blackmur has described it in his lecture, "Language as Gesture," after and as an effect of verbalization. The physiological process of speech-forming, as characterized in the passage quoted, is not meant to represent just a stage of human evolution; it is assumed to go on perpetually in the human being, to form the basis of human language where meanings undeniably exist, but are considered irrelevant. From this conjectural actualization and perpetuation of the evolutionary process, it is concluded that meanings, "shadows of images," no longer control a sentence, they are carried along, "slurred" into a motion that of itself determines its sense. We have arrived at the lowest conceivable level of association, association no longer of images of the unconscious, no longer of clashing conceptual word images—"mutual reflexes like flashes over jewels"—nor through the sound linkage of meanings, but association through "gestics," motion per se.

Now human language is not an oral ballet. It starts, whatever may be said, with "imagination," forming of

images, signs, meanings, with the simplest grasp of connections and coherences, with all that makes it possible to
be something more than dog, pig or rooster, but rather to
put oneself in another's place and thus establish a relationship with a psychic and mental opposite. Human language
springs from incipient consciousness and aims at a respond-
ing, corresponding consciousness. By expressing something,
it implicitly tends to move some one to some effect. Therefore, it cannot be shoved along by a sheer self-directed
motion; it is always directed by the urge or the will of a
human being.

The following pictures Franz Mon's conception of the
beginnings of articulation. It is entitled *From What You
Evolve (Aus was du wirst)*:[9]

```
rakon tsiste himil kokard reche chrest sukzess arb
  hakon  tris  umir  kott  ädre  rest  kukt  abe
  acre  dress  umsens  gorf  eder  kest  schuga
    kran  drett  rums  gror  dree  kir  sus
      krakä  dreis  rirn  grett  erd  rich
        kras  erk  ir  egs  rnd  re
          kars  ese  rir  rd  r
           hare  ids  urnd  hn
            arr  drie  odt  runn
              tror      unds
               tar      usd
                drustar
```

The geometrical arrangement of this piece shows the
transition to the *third,* lettristic and typographical, stage of
the literary avant-garde movement.

To be sure, these scriptural figurations also have their history and antecedents which, however, were intended to carry some playful meaning. Apollinaire's *Calligrammes,* for instance, which he sent home from the war, were fancies of consolation. The graphic ordering of the words accentuates the message of the writing. In the poem *Il pleut,* the arrangement of words in streamlines of rain reflect the rain of memories recounted in the poem. In another piece, the crossing of the word columns in a figure X pictures the separation of the lovers. The "calligrammes" of the present literary avant-gardes, however, are purely scriptural.

In general, the products of the manifold projecting theories of the avant-gardes hardly add anything substantial to the neologistic proclamations; they actually coincide with them. They are, in the words of Pierre Boulez, *"des horaires fictifs de trains qui ne partiront point,"* timetables for trains that will not depart. In following up this movement from stage to stage, we realize how increasing reduction turns into regression; progression consists in regression. The detachment of language from its human source leads, through the shrinking of verbality to "gestics," through the gradual decomposition of language into its components, and its merging in its phonic and graphic adjuncts, to its final evaporation in silence and the void.

Indeed, in the typographical arrangement of avant-garde texts, the *empty space* has a prominent role. It is the area, the "world" in which the "gestic" dislocations of words and letters take place. The words, word particles, letters are irregularly distributed over the surface, on different levels, in different distances and positions, and in the empty interspace between them, associations, or rather infinite potentialities of associations, are felt dormant, in suspense. Not even the last remnants of literality appear to be needed for such imaginary figurations to happen. "Even a scrap of paper," Mon suggests, "hit by a few splashes of water, is a reading field; the delicate shadows, the tiny traces on the surface are enough to make it readable . . . they suffice to put us on the scent of unknown, suggestive articulations. During the concentration of reading, this piece of paper represents . . . the world . . . a coordination that, with its left and right, above and below, tight and wide, curved and straight . . . reflects the orientation of our body."[10] The world, as you see, is a delimited void.

This notion brings to mind Taoistic thinking and painting, where also a particular capacity is attributed to emptiness. But in the Chinese concept the void represents "the creative entirety and potentiality of primeval origins."[11] In Mallarmé's *Coup de dés* the empty spaces between the printed words indicate pauses meant to enhance particular stresses within a quasi-musical flux of ideas. In our recent situation, however, no creative whole, no cosmic origin, no substantive meaning is seen behind the void. The void is what it is, sheer emptiness. And the associative possibilities, infinitely indefinite, dissolve into the vacuum that is supposed to create them.

The *musical* avant-gardes show striking parallels. Again,

what is prescribed is a psychological turn that implies, in the words of John Cage, "giving up everything that belongs to humanity," and "opening the doors of the music to the sounds that happen to be in the environment."[12] One has to realize that "sounds occur whether intended or not" and to turn "in the direction of those he does not intend." Composers should "give up the desire to control sound, clear [their] mind of music and set about discovering means to let sounds be themselves rather than vehicles for man-made theories or expressions of human sentiments." To be sure, John Cage states explicitly that, for a musician, "giving up everything that belongs to humanity" is equivalent to "giving up music."

Significantly, John Cage only talks of sounds; the word "tone" does not occur in his discussions. Indeed, sounds are to be clearly distinguished from tones. Sounds are isolated phenomena, natural phenomena. They may be made into tones when they are formed and transformed into a coherent order by a human intellectual act, a human effort that is a basic attribute of art, and that distinguishes art from the purposeless, laborless creations of nature. Now music specifically differs from the verbal and the plastic arts in that its very substratum is coherence, coherence per se. A word isolated and defunct as it may be, remains a word, something that conveys some meaning, something an immemorial effort of a human being has formed to express himself. A painting, be it ever so incoherent, is still a painting, made up of material stuff, colors and lines. But music without coherence is simply non-existent, unimaginable, for music *consists* in coherence, the ordered relationship of tones. An unrelated tone, a tone in itself is no longer a tone, it is just a sound; it is made into a tone through "composition," the traditional and the individually conceived order of rhythm, pitch, duration, intensity, and combinative color, an order into which human meanings and feelings flow, anonymously as it were. The avant-garde, however, is concerned plainly "with the co-existence of dissimilars," as John Cage puts it, ". . . not an attempt to bring order out of chaos, nor to suggest improvements in creation, but simply a way of waking up to the very life we're living, which is so excellent once one gets one's mind and one's desires out of its way and lets it act of its own accord."

To be sure, any sounds "may occur," John Cage states, "in any combination and in any continuity." Only these combinations are unable to produce any order and meaning, and as far as they arouse any human feelings at all, they are extraneous reactions, such as all sounds of nature may evoke; they are not comparable to the inmost feelings inherent in the creations of an artist.

The equivalent to Franz Mon's "emptiness" with its infinite potential associations is John Cage's "silence" which, to be sure, he finds never complete— "there is no such thing as an empty space or an empty time. There is

[91]

always something to see, something to hear." Even in an "anechoic chamber," a room without echoes, the sounds of one's own nervous system in operation and one's blood in circulation are audible. In such basic "silence," chance combination of noises and sounds correspond to Franz Mon's potential associations. "Until I die," John Cage says, "there will be sounds. And they will continue following my death." Surprisingly he concludes from this: "One need not fear about the future of music."

Finally, here again technology has its omnipotent part: "We are, in fact," John Cage triumphantly proclaims, "technically equipped to transform our contemporary awareness of nature's manner of operation into art. . . . Given four film phonographs, we can compose and perform a quartet for explosive motor, wind, heartbeat, and landslide."

The avant-gardes declare their movements to be the only ones fitting our technological age, and they may be right in maintaining that. Not only do they make ample use of mechanical techniques, but their unbounded functionality equals that of a dominant technology that pursues its unending ends of constructing and refining abstract objects without giving much thought to their human, that is, their non-functional implications. As far as the present avant-gardes are avant-gardes at all, they join with their various novelties formations which we find everywhere at work today. I do not venture to say what it is, that is helped into being aimlessly and unawares. Quite evident, however, appear to me the dangerous consequences of these developments for the future of humanity. They constitute an ultimate threat to human communication, or better, to the human element in the communication between man and man.

For a long time, human communication could be seen shifting from a discourse between the centers of inner life, that is, between people as human beings, to dealings between their functional peripheries, their occupational concerns. This has been noticeable in the ever-growing preponderance of specialized activities and endeavors, which extends into daily life. What it involves may be gathered from the example of the *transformations of reason*. The commonly human faculty of reason, popularized in the term "common sense," has been expanded and rarified into manifold scientific and technical rationality—to a point where, due to a failing of broader coherence, original reason and functional rationality have become sheer opposites. In this process, functional rationality has gained the upper hand so as to displace human reason. Scholars and scientists, who in their research control most intricate rational operations, may be seen sometimes lacking all sense of reason when faced with issues of general human import. Those 600 medical, or rather anti-medical scientists at Fort Detrick in Maryland who prepare the most devilish kinds of genocide, the physical and chemical engineers who work on the refinement of nuclear weapons, the military planners, the "think tanks" who have calculated all rationally foreseeable circumstances and tell us that, given adequate protective measures like getting used to spending our lives in fashionable caves, not the *whole* nation would perish in a third world war, but only a mere 60 to 100 million people —such experts, if confronted with the question of broadly human implications, would answer, with the pride of their professional amorality: "These matters exceed our competence; what we are concerned with are purely technical, rational problems." Limitation to strictly specialistic concerns has become a foremost intellectual virtue, and thus technical rationality serves universal potentialities which human reason must regard as patent madness and as monstrous crimes against humanity.

Now the avant-gardes, by severing language from human expression, not only work in the same direction, they make of this schism an explicit program. As indicated before, human language, by conveying some human impulse, be it a feeling, an experience, or a thought, tends to effect something, to affect human beings. Expression and aim are one. Hence, if language is divorced from human expression, it ceases to serve human aims. The experiments of the avant-gardes neither convey nor aim at anything human. They have established a new kind of artless, scientifically tinged *l'art pour l'art*. And even more radically than other intellectual activities they contribute to the atrophy of human concerns in human beings.

But this is not all. What these movements ultimately arrive at, what in the end they want to accomplish is the total *destruction of coherence,* and with it the deliberate, and that means, the *conscious destruction of consciousness.* Consciousness, I said, is awareness of coherence. Since its inception, art has been concerned with the creation of form, it has been an effort to achieve form, and that is, to seek out some coherence in reality—not necessarily rational coherence, but rather transrational, suprarational, or even subrational coherence, new coherence forming beneath the decay of the old. Whether the coherence an artist is striving for is rational or non-rational, objective or non-objective, tonal, atonal, or pantonal, is irrelevant in regard to the artistic authenticity of his work; the criterion is the achievement of new form, and the striving for it. To be sure, this criterion is more difficult to discern today than previously when the frontier of artistic endeavor lay within the area of our daily experience, when objects and happenings quite familiar to our senses provided a touchstone for our appreciation. However, as long as we sense in a work that effort, that captive road toward the achievement of a coherence, as long as we can retrace in the work this striving to disclose the innermost structure of phenomenality, or to express an innermost, most delicate psychic experience, we feel assured of its artistic authenticity and can re-live a creative process. Indeed, as we have seen, even in the rendering of a totality of existence with all its disparate constituents, even in the attempt to assemble a totality of motley debris, we may notice a paradoxical intention to show some coherence in incoherence. But from the moment when the unconscious itself became the enactor of the artistic process, the achievement of coherence and implicitly the effort to achieve it vanished.

So the next stage of the development is the outspoken attempt to *produce incoherence,* incoherence as such, devoid of any cause or purpose. What we witness all round is a veritable cult of incoherence, of sheer senselessness and aimlessness. We find it in writings, in paintings and decorations, in "chance" or "aleatory composing," in the mad contortions of the latest dances, in the Beatle frenzies, the fancy dress bearing of the Hippies, in the organized mischief of the Dutch Provos, the Californian Hell's Angels, the Japanese Zero Dimension Group—to mention just a few of these youth gatherings. Of course these are just so many ways of protest, of conscious or unconscious statements of not-belonging to our conventional society. Among the Hippies and particularly their youngest generations, the "Diggers," an aim at a new form of community, of living together, is gaining force, but so far the place where it establishes itself is the chimeric, quietistic, inconsequential world of psychedelics.

The foremost manifestations of the cult of incoherence are the *happenings,* those celebrations of artificial accidentalness, in which audiences are spectators and at the same time victims of a random mixture of trivial and eccentric acts and occurrences—the issue being the production of the unexpected. (In Rauschenberg's highly technological happening, the mechanical stunts did not function, which does not make so much difference because the non-functioning may be just what was not to be expected.) The perpetual production of unexpectables, however, is gradually wearing off, and the unexpected ends up in being just the expected. So the happenings are more and more radicalized to a point where they turn into performances of sheer destruction, which is called "creative vandalism." In London the first "International Destruction in Art" Symposium convened. All sorts of objects were wrecked, and the French *groupe panique* went so far as to crucify a live chicken. Such an extreme of enacted incoherence reflects the mood of a desolate youth discouraged from aims, and informed by the unremitting lesson of reckless official violence.

All the movements we have discussed here and have seen evolving from afar are brought to a climax of active confusion by that intellectual demagogue, Marshall McLuhan. He started out by recognizing correctly the symptoms of a condition that makes life increasingly unlivable for human beings. But instead of seeking a remedy through patient coordination that could bring ineluctable developments back under human control, he is swept along by his findings to enthusiastic affirmation, reminiscent of that French police captain who said: *"Je suis leur chef, il faut que je les suive"* (I am their chief, I have to follow them). By radicalizing the trends of our youth, McLuhan won the support of quite a number of educational institutions who take his "probings" at face value, most conspicuously—of all places—a Catholic university whose tenets could not be more contradictory to what he propagates.

He diagnoses the dwindling of all substance in the functionalization of all our activities by stating that it is the medium that absorbs all import. But he drives it to the absurd by generalization. "War is total education because it sends an entire society into action." The total mobilization of a people in the First World War, which really involved the whole society—as described by Ernst Jünger—was at least done for a wrong nationalistic purpose, and it resulted in the Third Reich of the Nazis. Today, according to McLuhan, it is irrelevant to ask: education for what? And it is irrelevant to specify what is meant by "action." Let it be the worst of violence, corruption, and atrocity, let it be the death of a whole people. If we realize that it is an all-out educational effort, we shall "abandon our disgust" and shall swallow the consequences. The medium is the message.

The trend of the recent generations is, as we have seen, toward emphasis on the present and presence. From pop art and the *nouveau roman* to behaviorism and the structuralist similes of Lévy-Strauss, the wind levels down evolutional stages and reduces our vista to the sight of the moment. The complexity and overcrowding of our factual knowledge have made it discontinuous and unmasterable. The turmoil of multiplied and accelerated events in which we are living, the pace of technological exploits, the omnipresence of our entire globe in the news, drive our feeling of existence to the point of simultaneity. It is more than understandable that our youth loathes the bookish record of things and is incapable of uncovering the thread of life under the heaps of material. So they turn outward to the tangible life of the senses and exchange the cumbersome discontinuity of learning for the fleeting discontinuity of the mass of impressions, that is, the classroom for television. Being unable to understand the wilderness of phenomena, they indulge in it or try to escape from this world through what goes under the name of "expansion of consciousness," the timeless, placeless, hallucinatory intensification of perception through drugs. This is where Timothy Leary joins hands with Marshall McLuhan.

Irresponsibly, McLuhan fosters this chaotic development. His sophistry, as all sophistry, makes use of linguistic confusion. He confounds consciousness—which is awareness of coherence—with perception, which is its raw material. The trend toward simultaneity, on which the various processes of our life converge, can be brought under control, that is, to coordination, only through synthesis, not through accumulation, through a view from a distance, not through immediate participation. Television, McLuhan says, has created a huge gap between generations who learned to read and write before TV and those who came to TV first. The TV generation, he states, because it is accustomed to an outer environment, "charged with messages," is in rebellion against the print-oriented school system. This movement, if pursued without direction, must lead to practical illiteracy, indeed to the "retribalization" viewed so approvingly by McLuhan. It could be guided into productive channels only through a fundamental change in our management of TV and our educational outlook. It is ridiculous to contend, as McLuhan does, that the young generations watch television because of their want of "depth and involvement." They watch television for the sensuous pleasure in the happening as such, be it even the variety of commercials, and for the vicarious indulgence in violence which is so abundantly displayed in the programs. To call that "involvement" is a euphemistic connivance. What they seek is pure surface, the opposite of depth.

It is true that the perpetual presence of the world, the close interrelation of events, and the demands of democracy potentially involve us in the destinies of humanity. We are all responsible for whatever happens in the world, and a guideless feeling of this stirs the intellectual youth. But this involvement remains entirely passive because of the manipulation of our democracy and the very increase of illiteracy among the "TV generation."

It is certainly not commercial television, whose orgies of idiocy entertain the masses, that could answer the true needs of our youth; nor is it even educational television in its present form, which offers only selected and incoherent bits from our cultural stock or from the body of science that, to be enjoyed, presuppose some interest and taste developed by reading. What could make instruction palatable—and committal—for the young would be a combination of visual and verbal, discursive education which in television and in the classroom would convey to them a total picture of our contemporary world and show them the so-called historical past as simply the roots of our present situation. It would present opportunities for discussion of the problems of the day, which could create real involvement. This is a novel task that good teachers doubtlessly grapple with already, but that would have to be taken up with methodical care. It would not be possible without gross simplification, particularly in trying to make modern complex processes visually understandable. But even such simplification would be preferable to what happens now, under the influence of McLuhan's erratic "probings."

It is life as discotheque. "A new exhibition hall at

Toronto's Royal Ontario Museum, designed by Harvey Parker, the museum's director and an associate of Marshall McLuhan . . . employs multimedia techniques and allows visitors to participate in a 'multisensual experience' created by slide projections and color cartoons, flashing lights, sounds of gulls and thunder, and fossils they can feel." "The new communication techniques," say multimedia theoreticians, "take into account the daily bombardment of our senses by an extraordinary multiplicity of stimuli. . . . Electric-media theater events by Aldo Tamburini, an artist, are not played by conventional actors. Instead they are blitzed by such devices as eye-searing strobe-lights, wailing sirens, the jumpy play of images on a screen, and a huge balloon that bursts with the clap of a thunderbolt. 'We are the primitives of a new era,' says Mr. Tamburini. 'With multimedia you create an effect that is not based on previous experience. You saturate the audience with images. It happens now—it has a live quality. It's a total experience in itself.' "

The result is, we are told, "that the re-creation in a heightened, intensified way, of complex environmental experiences can *expand our consciousness* to *higher levels of perception*. In fact, multimedia artists like the USCO— the US company, a 'tribe' of artist-engineers . . . believe that overloading the senses until *rational judgment and choice are blocked* may greatly enhance the impact of what is communicated."[13]

Here dehumanization has reached the physical constitution of man. The daily environmental situation which metropolitan residents have to bear is nearing the limits of what the human sensorium can stand. Doctors have established the damages that excessive noises cause in people's nervous condition. The building of suprasonic jet planes on a large scale, which our wise government has granted first priority, can be expected to widen these damages to an unbearable degree. While exposed to the environmental mingling of sensations, as it exists in our big cities today, the mind defends itself by suppressing automatically as much as possible the unusable or unwelcome noises and visions into the unconscious, to make room for the acts of consciousness. If the sensations become obtrusive, the mind seeks to escape and to put an end to that annoying condition. This unavoidable evil of metropolitan life can hardly present a desirable model for the artificial creation of a situation where all the multiple sensations through extreme intensification claim an inescapable simultaneous attention. It admittedly "blocks all rational judgment and choice." Far from "expanding consciousness," it explodes it, drives it out of our senses into numbness, into an insensate state of perpetual panic. Do these devotees of McLuhan's really have to be told what they could learn from simple physical observation, that overloading causes explosion, and that perception is not identical with consciousness? It would indeed require a change of the psysiological condition of the human being to make a state of multisensory perception continually tolerable, and it would still not produce an enlargement of consciousness, i.e., a larger scope of understanding coherence.

Again the question arises: for what? To heighten the already disastrous anarchy? The only use it has concretely shown is its effect on business advertising which benefits from the benumbing of consciousness. The Scott Paper Company reported a sales increase of eleven per cent as a result of multidimensional presentations that culminated in the promotion of a product that had been difficult to sell. So the whole array of bombastic preparations ends up where everything ends up nowadays in this country: making money.

In conclusion, let me briefly consider the present condition and the prospects of *poetry,* this most intense form of human communication. The avant-gardes hardly use the word "poetry" any longer, and rightly so. Their products go under a variety of names, the most common among them is "texts." Anyway, poetry, true poetry still exists in spite of the recent tendencies to dissolve non-functional language; but—and how could it be otherwise—poetry too is affected by the general disintegration of form and devaluation of feeling.

Now poetry is based on feeling. Even its rendering of very concrete experience, or of very abstract contemplation, must be borne along by feeling to move its audience to the specifically poetic effect, that focal illumination of existence, "that heightened, that excited sense of being," as Richard Blackmur put it, from which it sprang. The radical extraversion, the phenomenal and psychic complexity of our life, and hence the manifold jargonization and trivialization of language have brought about a scattering of sentiments into multifarious peripheral sensibilities, a kind of subtle analytical sentience. Minds who are sensitive to language, to whom the magic of the spoken word is quite real, are repelled by overused phrases, too flat to express a unique personal experience in a unique human situation. The devaluation of words reflects on the feeling behind them, and in this way sentiment comes to be identified with sentimentality, which actually is inflated, corrupted, conventionalized sentiment. The uncertainty of language often produces an uncertainty of feeling. People ask themselves: Do I really feel? Is it worth feeling?

This is the process that compels what there is of true sentiment to escape into the anonymity of the factual, to disperse into minute sensibilities kindled by incidental experiences; or to flow hidden in satire, or in cryptically remote and compressed metaphorics. Of course, any genuine poem is cryptic, venturing as it does at the frontiers of the expressible. But the new kind of metaphoric contraction is cryptic through the remoteness of sensibility, which is the result of ineluctable linguistic fastidiousness and emotional reserve.

Often we see poetry degenerate into sheer factual statement, into the narrative cursed by Mallarmé and into hacked prose—bad prose at that, since such fettered prose is prevented from following its own peculiar rhythms. Not only inept scribblers resort to such misuses, but occasionally even genuine, important poets, like Robert Lowell in his *Life Studies*. The poem "My Last Afternoon with Uncle Devereux," for instance, renders superbly the atmosphere and flavor of Lowell's home scene. But why did it have to be versified?

Let us not forget what a poem is, what distinguishes poetry from prose: not meters, not lines cut by enjambements, but a different kind of language. A poem is, always has been, a communication which a genuine urge, the immediate impulse of experience, be it a flash of lucidity, delight, or suffering, raises quite naturally to a language more intense, more concentrated, more vibrant than prose, which never belies its musical, "lyrical" origin; a language spontaneously gliding into its rhythms, of which meters are but the appropriate divisions. Such sublimation of language has nothing to do with loftiness, uplift, or verbal rarefication. The elevated tone may carry everyday, even slangy language, and even in its most daring innovations it must remain the authentic expression of the poet, an essentialization of his normal speech; or, to put it in reverse, the poet must in his daily life be innately capable of such elevation. The authenticity or falseness of the tone shows unmistakably.

The poetic form is not arbitrarily applicable to any "content." What can be said in prose should not be forced into verse. Only something that cannot be said otherwise than poetically is worthy of verse, indeed produces real verse, which is but the form of expression of heightened experience. Even when poets like Brecht or Peter Weiss in his *Investigation* are using verse for factual reporting, this is done in a reversed, sardonic sense, for the sake of sharpening a repelling contrast with what is said. But here again it is the poetic urge that determines the form.

This does not mean that such an indispensable urge is all that is needed to create a true poem. The full realization of a poem requires work, hard work sometimes. "The lord and master," Valéry said, "has given you the spark, it is your task to make something of it." The problems of this "making"—methods and style—have to be pondered and discussed, but, for poetry to remain true poetry, the "making" should never predominate in the poem, poetry should never become professional, as it tends to be so frequently today.

We have still among us, in all countries, genuine, even great poets, voices of humanity in the midst of mounting dehumanization. But given the all-pervading blind emulation of science and technology which tend to monopolize the human purpose without being capable of establishing such a purpose, of providing us some guidance for the conduct of our life, we may seriously question whether poetry will be able to maintain itself much longer amidst "ultra-intelligent machines." How long will it be left time and space and a natural soil in which to grow in young people. We see the poetic urge arise from inner revolt in oppressed countries, we still sense it breaking through the political and intellectual thicket in the distress and rebellion of Western poets. But it is high time, I believe, to warn our youth, and encourage and support those among them who already are aroused, against that grave, that vital danger: the overall dominance of scientism, that is, of scientistic mentality (to be distinguished from true science itself, its inestimable value, though not limitless validity); to warn them of that current inclination to see all of our life, indeed all reality, as a complex of detectable, ultimately predictable and reproducible "mechanisms."

We live in a chaotic world, overcrowded with people, objects and techniques, torn by conflicts and corruptions, overshadowed by perils of unprecedented dimensions. The general anarchy is enhanced by the analytic temper which proliferates boundlessly all over our life, part of which is what appears to be the most futile of all, the methodical wrecking of human language. We are confronted with an ever increasing mass of unmastered life-material, without and within ourselves. What we must do today above all, it seems to me, is to gather all our resources for the mastery of our world, which means directing our efforts toward establishing rather than dissevering and dissecting co-herences. The sciences find it difficult to make such an effort in their own way. They cannot help growing more and more specialized, they are forced in their research to proceed analytically. Advance of material knowledge calls for analysis. The sciences would have to enlist the aid of the synoptical faculties of art, whose function has always been to concentrate, to distil the essence out of phenomenality, to seek integration through intuitive vistas, to see things in perspective and as wholes. From new experiences, from the exertion to express them with utmost and inmost accuracy, ever new language evolves.

Mastery means form. Form, developing from whatever material through unhurried, laborious care, is the last sanctuary of human expression, our last defense against the onslaught of technocratic slogans and against the boundless analytical arguings that threaten to smother the human voice.

THE TRIUMPH OF INCOHERENCE

Illustrations

Writers' and Painters' Scriptural Figurations
Illustrative and Purely Scriptural Literary Calligrammes
Empty Space

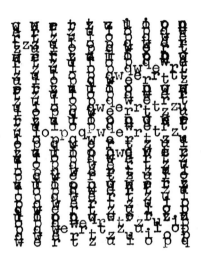

Franz Mon, "Schreibmaschinentextbild"

Reproduced from Schrift und Bild, *Typos Verlag, Frankfurt,*
copyright © *1963*

Franz Mon, "Abstraktion"

Reproduced from Schrift und Bild, *Typos Verlag, Frankfurt,*
copyright © *1963*

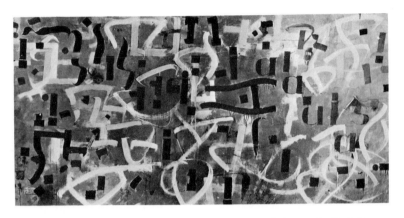

Bradley Tomlin, "Number 9: In Praise of Gertrude Stein"
(1950)
Collection, The Museum of Modern Art, New York
Gift of Mrs. John D. Rockefeller, 3rd

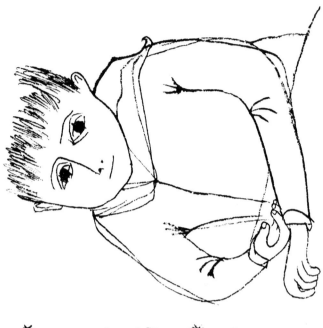

Ben Shahn, "Who Is God?"

WHO IS GOD? WELL IT IS AN INVISIBLE PERSON AND HE LIVES UP IN HEAVEN I GUESS UP IN OUTER SPACE HE MADE THE EARTH AND THE HEAVEN & THE STARS AND THE SUN AND THE PEOPLE HE MADE LIGHT HE MADE DAY HE MADE NIGHT HE HAS SUCH POWERFUL EYES HE DOESN'T HAVE MILLIONS AND THOUSANDS AND BILLIONS AND HE CAN STILL SEE US WHEN WE'RE BAD HE STARTED ALL THE PLANTS GROWING TO ME I THINK OF HIM WHO MAKES FLOWERS & GREEN GRASS & THE BLUE SKY & THE YELLOW SUN GOD IS EVERYWHERE & I DON'T KNOW HOW HE COULD DO IT

Ben Shahn, untitled composition

Reproduced from Love and Joy About Letters, *Grossman Publishers,*
New York, copyright © Ben Shahn, 1963

Mark Tobey, "Sumi Still Life" (1957)
Collection, Galerie Jeanne Bucher, Paris
Photo: Luc Joubert

Paul Klee, "Pinselzeichnung"

Reproduced from Schrift und Bild, *Typos Verlag, Frankfurt,*
copyright © *1963*

PAYSAGE

V
OI
CI LA **?** MAISON
Où NAISSENT
LES É
TOI LES
ET LES DIVINITÉS

CET
ARBRISSEAU
QUI SE PRÉPARE
A FRUCTIFIER
TE
RES
SEM
BLE

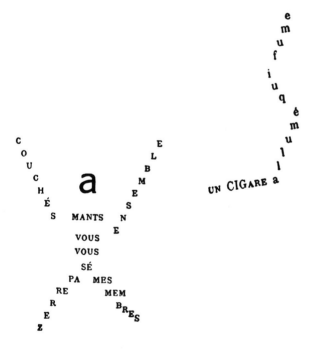

Guillaume Apollinaire, "Paysage"

IL PLEUT

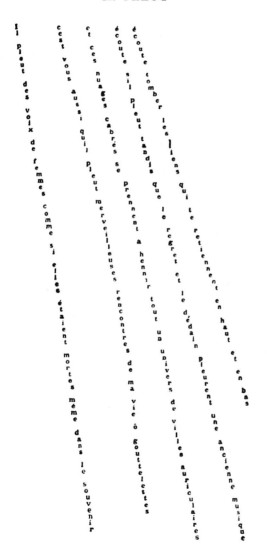

Guillaume Apollinaire, "Il Pleut"

Apollinaire Calligrammes, *Editions Gallimard, Paris,*
copyright © *1925*

Klaus Peter Dienst, "Kalligramm"

Reproduced from Movens, *Typos Verlag, Frankfurt,*
copyright © *1960*

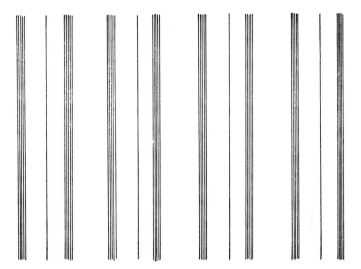

John Cage, "Notations for Chance Composition"

Reproduced from die Reihe #3, Musical Craftsmanship, *edited by Herbert Eimert and Karlheinz Stockhausen; German edition, copyright* © *1957, Universal Edition AG; English edition, copyright* © *1959, Theodore Presser Company, Philadelphia*

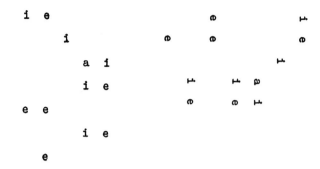

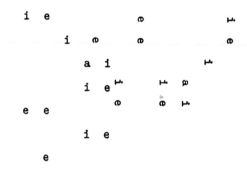

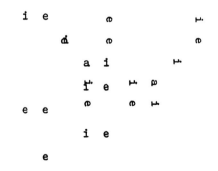

Carlfriedrich Claus, "6 Phasen Von 52"

Reproduced from Movens, *Typos Verlag, Frankfurt,*
copyright © *1960*

Diter Rot, untitled calligram

Reproduced from Movens, *Typos Verlag, Frankfurt,*
copyright © *1960*

References

LECTURE I: *The Forms of Form*

1. Aristotle, the *Poetics,* translated by Lane Cooper (rev. ed., Ithaca, 1947).
2. The following quotations from Matisse and Cézanne are taken from Robert Goldwater and Marco Treves, eds., *Artists on Art* (New York, 1945).
3. Thomas Hardy, quoted in Walter Allen, ed., *Writers on Writing* (New York, 1959).
4. Henry Miller, *Tropic of Cancer* (New York, 1961). Reprinted by permission of Grove Press, Inc.
5. Djuna Barnes, *Nightwood* (New York, 1946). Reprinted by permission of the author and New Directions Publishing Corporation.

LECTURE II: *The Preliminary Stages of Disintegration*

1. Nathalie Sarraute, *L'ère du soupçon* (Paris, 1952), pp. 10 ff. (The English edition, *The Age of Suspicion,* was published by George Braziller, New York, 1963.)
2. Pablo Picasso, quoted in Goldwater and Treves, eds., *op. cit.,* pp. 416 ff.

3. Franz Kafka, *Tagebücher* (September 23, 1912).
4. Pablo Picasso, quoted in Goldwater and Treves, eds., *op. cit,* pp. 416 ff.
5. The following quotations from Kline, Rothko, Okada, and Pollock are taken from Selden Rodman, *Conversations with Artists* (New York, 1961).
6. Allen Ginsberg, *Howl and Other Poems* (San Francisco, 1956).
7. William Burroughs, quoted in Seymour Krim, ed., *The Beats* (Greenwich, Connecticut, 1960).
8. Nathalie Sarraute, *op. cit.,* p. 11.
9. Hans Richter, *Dada-Kunst und Antikunst* (Cologne, 1964), pp. 210 ff.
10. Alain Robbe-Grillet, *Jealousy,* translated by Richard Howard (New York, 1959). Reprinted by permission of Grove Press, Inc.
11. Alain Robbe-Grillet, *For a New Novel, Essays on Fiction,* translated by Richard Howard (New York, 1965), pp. 21–24. Reprinted by permission of Grove Press, Inc.

LECTURE III: *The Triumph of Incoherence*

1. Stéphane Mallarmé, *Crise de vers* (Paris, Ed. de la Pléiade, 1951), p. 366.
2. *Ibid.,* p. 363.
3. Richard Huelsenbeck, *Dada, eine literarische Dokumentation* (Hamburg, 1964), pp. 9 ff.
4. Alfredo Giuliani, Introduction to *I Novissimi* (Milan, 1961), p. xiv.
5. *Ibid.,* pp. xvii ff.

6. Helmut Heissenbüttel, "Voraussetzungen," in Hans Bender, *Das Gedicht ist mein Messer, Lyriker zu ihren Gedichten* (2nd ed., Munich, 1961), pp. 89 ff.

7. Franz Mon, original English text from *Movens, Dokumente und Analysen zur Dichtung, bildenden Kunst, Musik, Architektur* (Wiesbaden, 1960), p. 189.

8. Franz Mon, *Artikulationen* (Pfullingen, 1959), pp. 31 ff.

9. Franz Mon, *Movens, op. cit.,* p. 113.

10. Franz Mon, *Artikulationen, op. cit.,* pp. 31 ff.

11. Tao Tê Ching, quoted in George Rowley, *Principles of Chinese Painting* (Princeton, 1947), p. 77.

12. This and the following quotations are from John Cage, *Silence* (Middletown, Connecticut, 1961), p. 3, pp. 7 ff.

13. *New York Times,* September 16, 1967, pp. 35, 37.

Index

Albee, Edward, 41
Apollinaire, Guillaume, 77, 88
Aristotle, 6f, 9
Arp, Hans, 79

Balzac, 10, 14
Barnes, Djuna, 17f
Barthes, Roland, 48
Baudelaire, 14
Beckmann, Max, 36f
Beethoven, 10
Benn, Gottfried, 16f, 43
Bense, Max, 81
Bergson, 19
Bissier, Julius, 79
Blackmur, Richard P., 21, 86, 105
Bosch, Hieronymus, 10
Boulez, Pierre, 88
Bourget, Paul, 33
Braque, 79
Brecht, 107

Breughel, 11
Broch, Hermann, 9
Burroughs, William, 44
Butor, Michel, 9

Cage, John, 40, 90–92
Cézanne, 8
Chekhov, 8f
Choderlos de Laclos, 29
Chopin, Henri, 80
Corso, Gregory, 77

Dante, 7
Dickens, 10
Dine, Jim, 45
Duckworth, George E., 7n
Du Deffand, Marie Anne, 30

Eliot, T. S., 17

Fichte, 31
Flaubert, 8, 13f, 39, 76
Fortlage, Karl, 32

Freud, 19, 34, 47

Gabo, Naum, 79
Garnier, Henri, 81
Gide, André, 9
Giedion, Siegfried, 22
Ginsberg, Allen, 44, 77
Giuliani, Alfredo, 83
Goethe, 8, 32
Gomringer, Eugen, 83*n*

Hardy, Thomas, 12*f*
Hegel, 31
Heissenbüttel, Helmut, 84
Hopkins, Gerard Manley, 14
Huelsenbeck, Richard, 77

Ibsen, 8*f*

James, Henry, 8
James, William, 34*f*
Janouch, Gustav, 38
Jean Paul (Friedrich Richter),
  32
Johnson, Uwe, 9
Joyce, 9, 76

Kafka, 37*f*
Kerouac, Jack, 44
Klee, 79
Kleist, Heinrich von, 8
Kline, Franz, 41
Kokoschka, 36*f*

La Fayette, Marie Madeleine
  de, 29
Langgässer, Elisabeth, 9
Leary, Timothy, 99
Lévi-Strauss, Claude, 99
Locke, 74
Lowell, Robert, 106

McLuhan, Marshall, 97–104
Mallarmé, 14, 75–77, 89, 105
Manessier, Alfred, 79
Mann, Thomas, 9
Marinetti, Filippo Tommaso,
  77*f*
Matisse, 8
Miller, Henry, 14*f*
Miró, 79
Mon, Franz, 84–87, 89, 91*f*
Mondrian, 79

Nicholson, Ben, 79
Nietzsche, 34
Novalis (Friedrich von Hard-
  enberg), 31

Okada, 40

Parker, Harvey, 102
Picasso, 38*f*
Plato, 7
Pollock, Jackson, 40*f*
Proust, 10, 35*f*

Rauschenberg, Robert, 97

Reinhardt, Ad, 42*f*

Richter, Hans, 44*f*

Riemer, Friedrich Wilhelm, 32

Rimbaud, 77

Robbe-Grillet, Alain, 45–49

Rothko, Mark, 40*f*

Rousseau, Jean Jacques, 30

Sarraute, Nathalie, 35*f*, 44

Schopenhauer, 32

Sénancour, Etienne Pivert de, 31

Shahn, Ben, 7.

Shakespeare, 11

Socrates, 7

Steinberg, Saul, 79

Stendhal, 31

Styron, William, 9

Tamburini, Aldo, 102

Teilhard de Chardin, 19

Thomas, Dylan, 14

Tobey, Mark, 79

Tolstoi, 8

Tomlin, Bradley Walker, 79

Valéry, 14, 107

van Gogh, 36*f*

Vergil, 7

Vieira da Silva, Maria Helena, 79

Walpole, Horace, 30

Webern, Anton von, 10

Weiss, Peter, 107

Whitman, Walt, 14, 77

Wittgenstein, 80

Wölfflin, Heinrich, 11

Woolf, Virginia, 9

Yeats, 8